Caroline's
Coloring Creations

Floral Fiesta

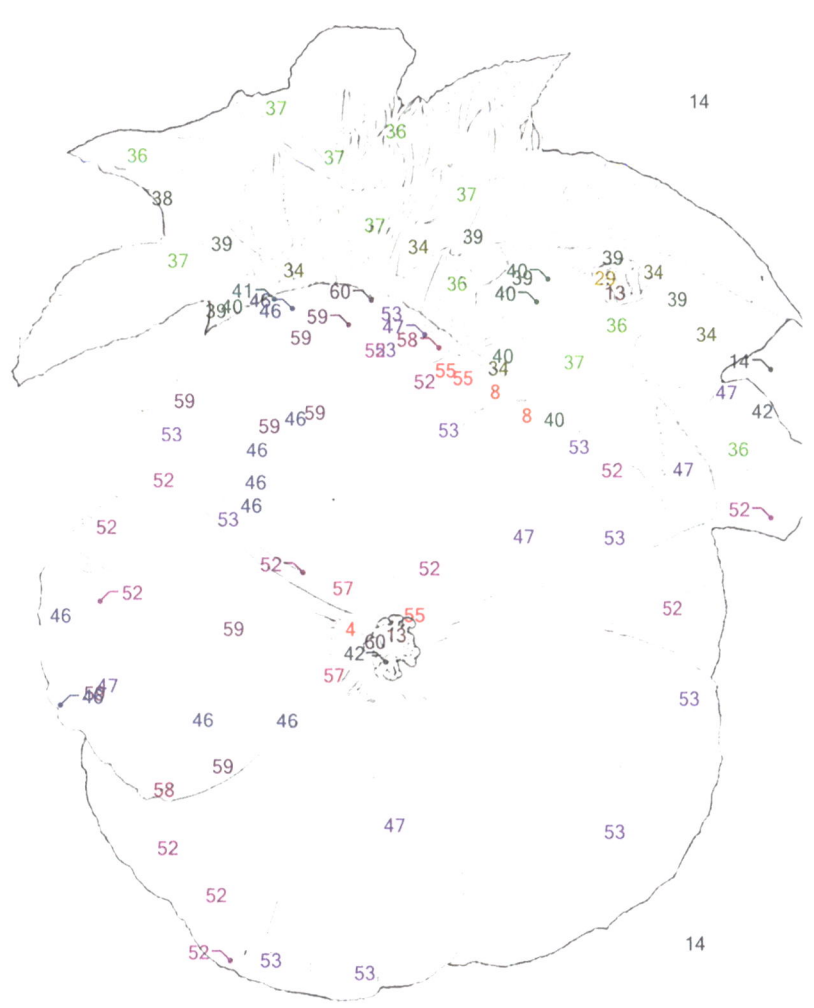

This is the first of a series of coloring books featuring my photography, adapted by processing software, into pictures for coloring. So that you can see the original photo compared with the potential coloring pages, I have purposely allowed the printing to be on both sides of the page. You are more than welcome to scan and print the pictures to color them.

As one who is a Christian and in Twelve Step Recovery, the phrases, "easy does it" and "one step at a time" were my daily tools used in keeping myself on task. It took patience in learning the process of transforming the photos, converting them to color by number and then to prep the new files to by press ready for publication. This work became a joy as I diligently plodded ahead and achieved my goal.

You will not that the color pencil graphics only have the corresponding numbers for coloring suggestions. To prevent any suggestion of copyright infringement, I did not name the colors.

Be on the lookout for the next in this series.

Enjoy

Caroline

1.
2. 2
3. 3
4. 4
5. 5
6. 6
7. 7
8. 8
9. 9
10. 10
11. 11
12. 12
13. 13
14. 14
15. 15
16. 16
17. 17
18. 18
19. 19
20. 20
21. 21
22. 22
23. 23

24. 24
25. 25
26. 26
27. 27
28. 28
29. 29
30. 30
31. 31
32. 32
33. 33
34. 34
35. 35
36. 36
37. 37
38. 38
39. 39
40. 40
41. 41
42. 42
43. 43
44. 44
45. 45
46. 46

47. 47
48. 48
49. 49
50. 50
51. 51
52. 52
53. 53

54. 54
55. 55
56. 56
57. 57
58. 58
59. 59
60. 60

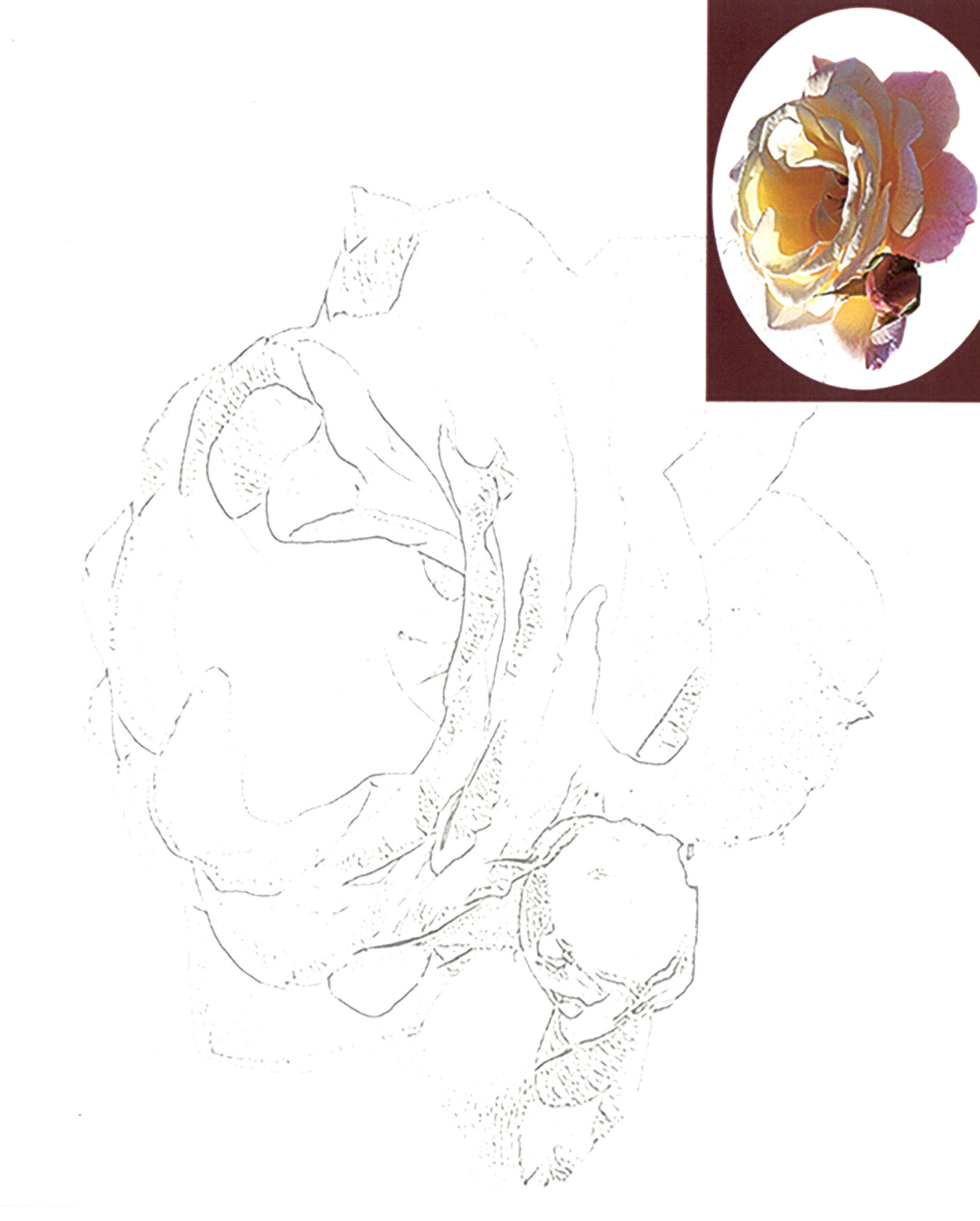

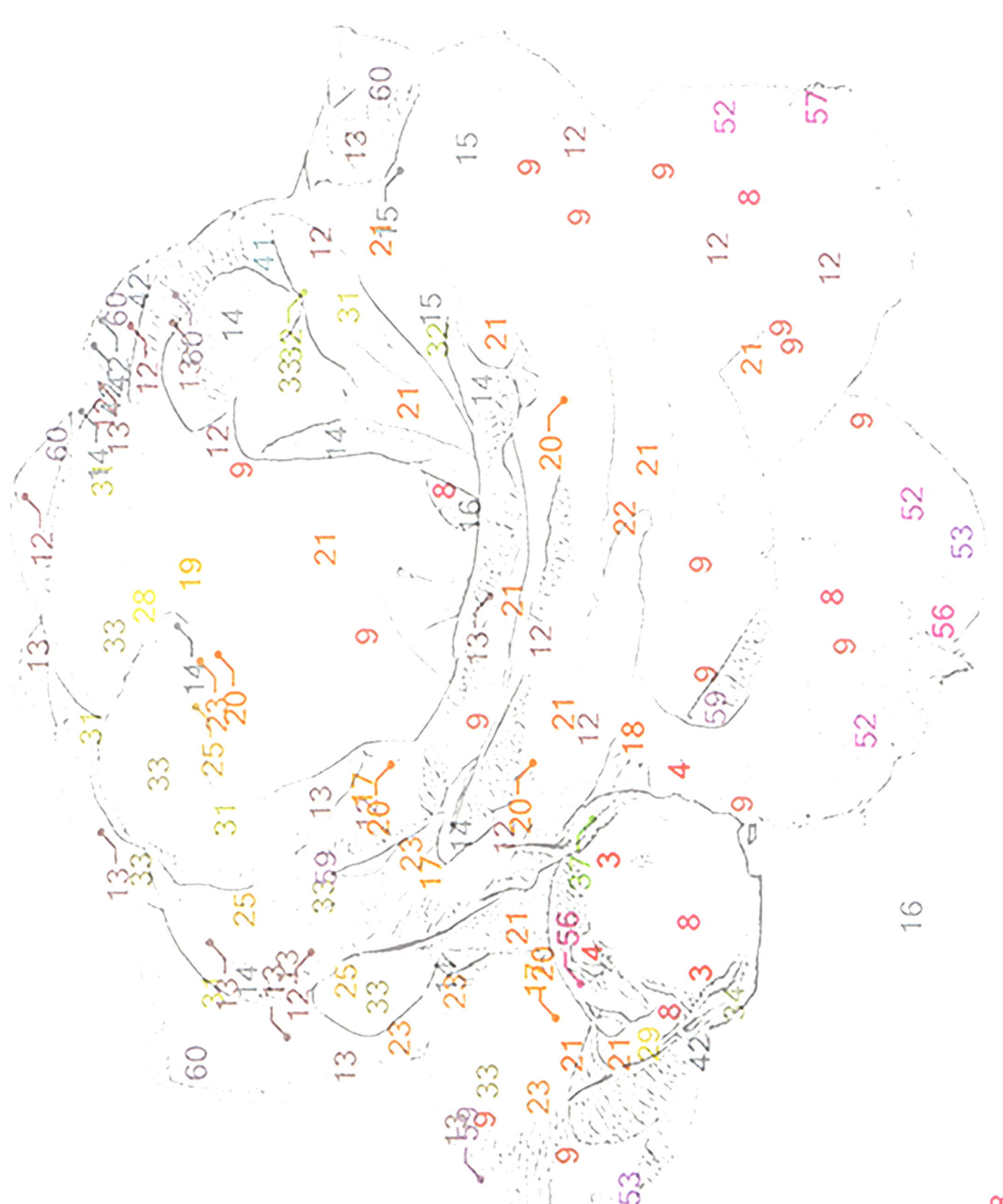

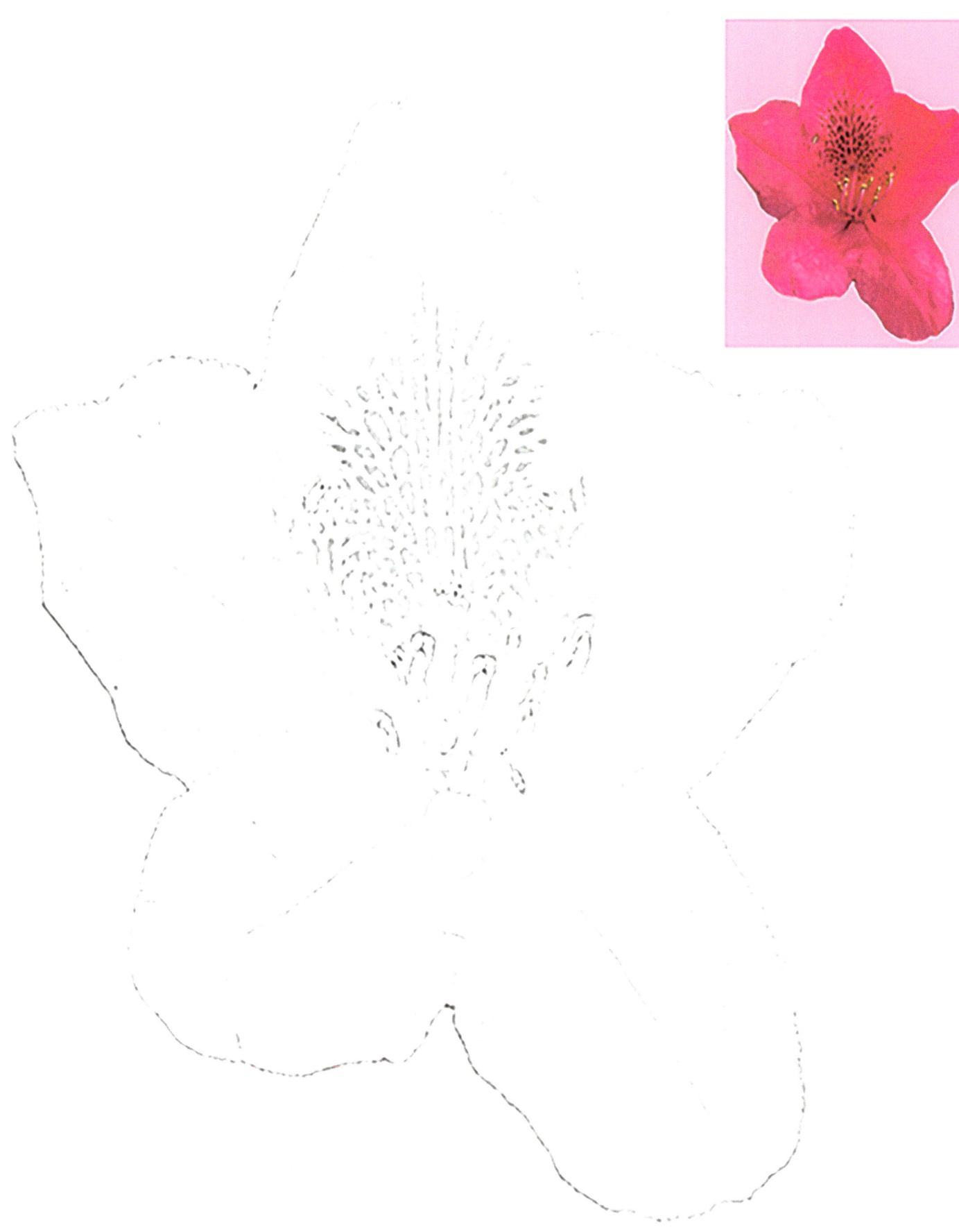

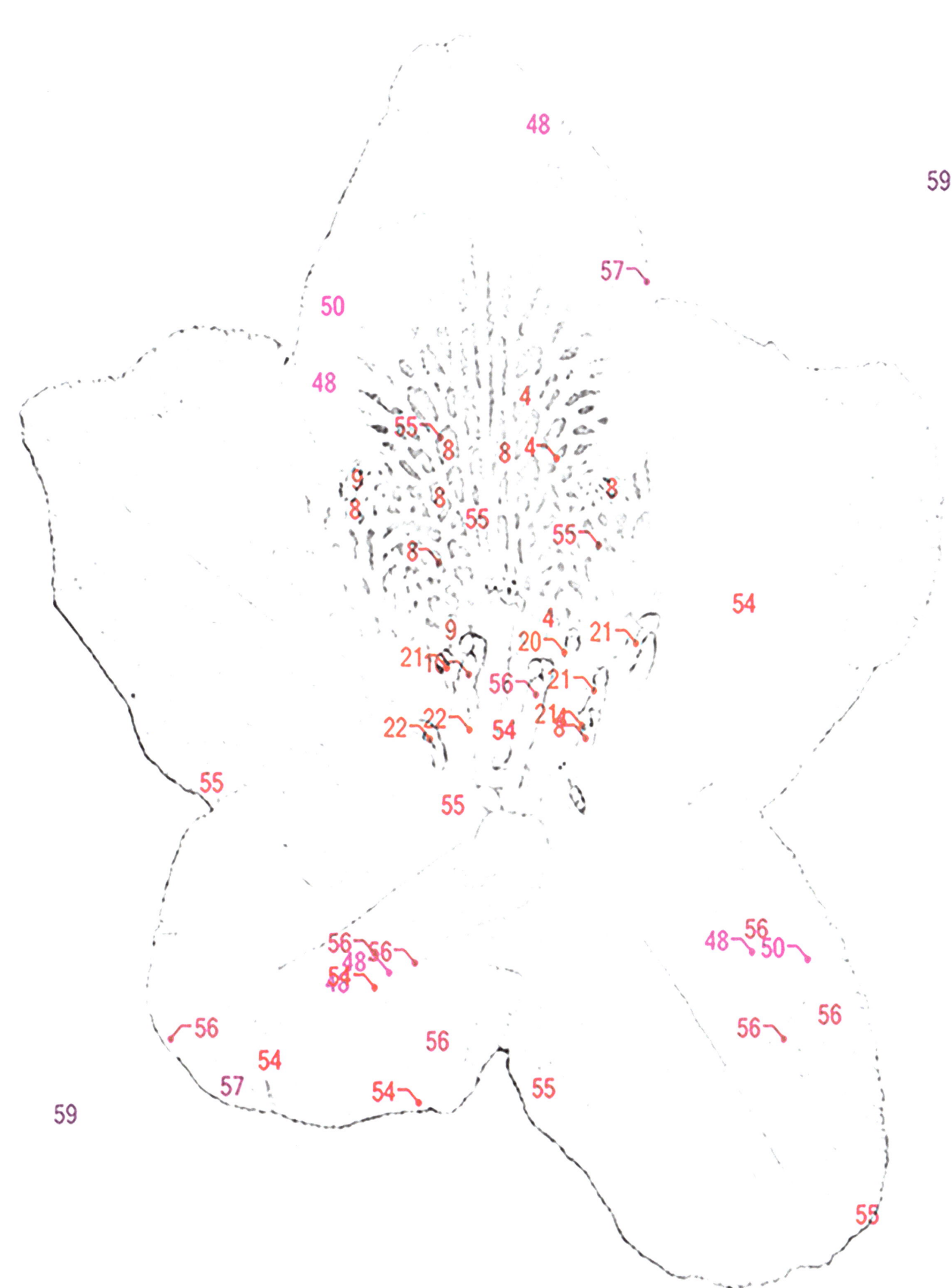

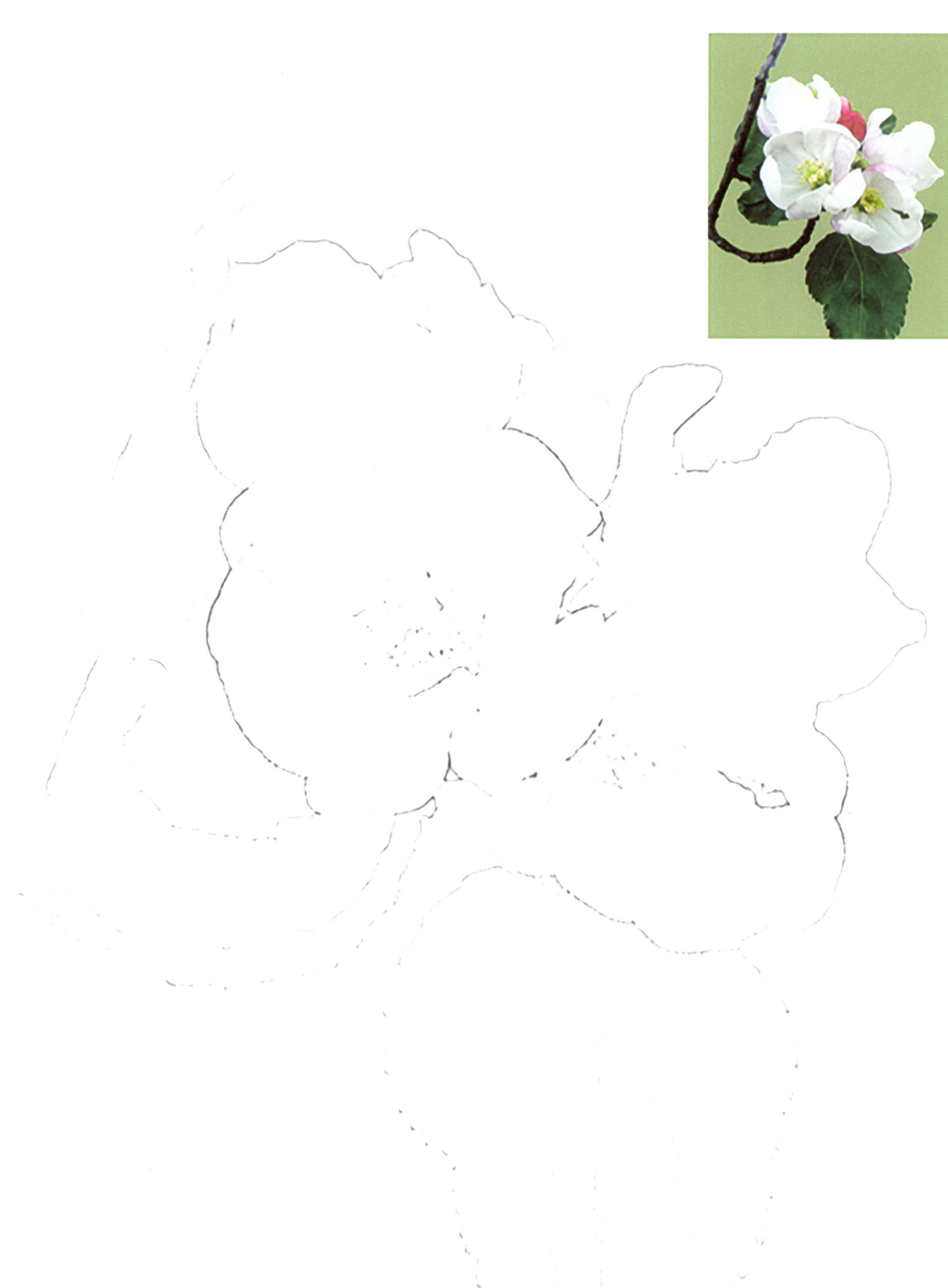

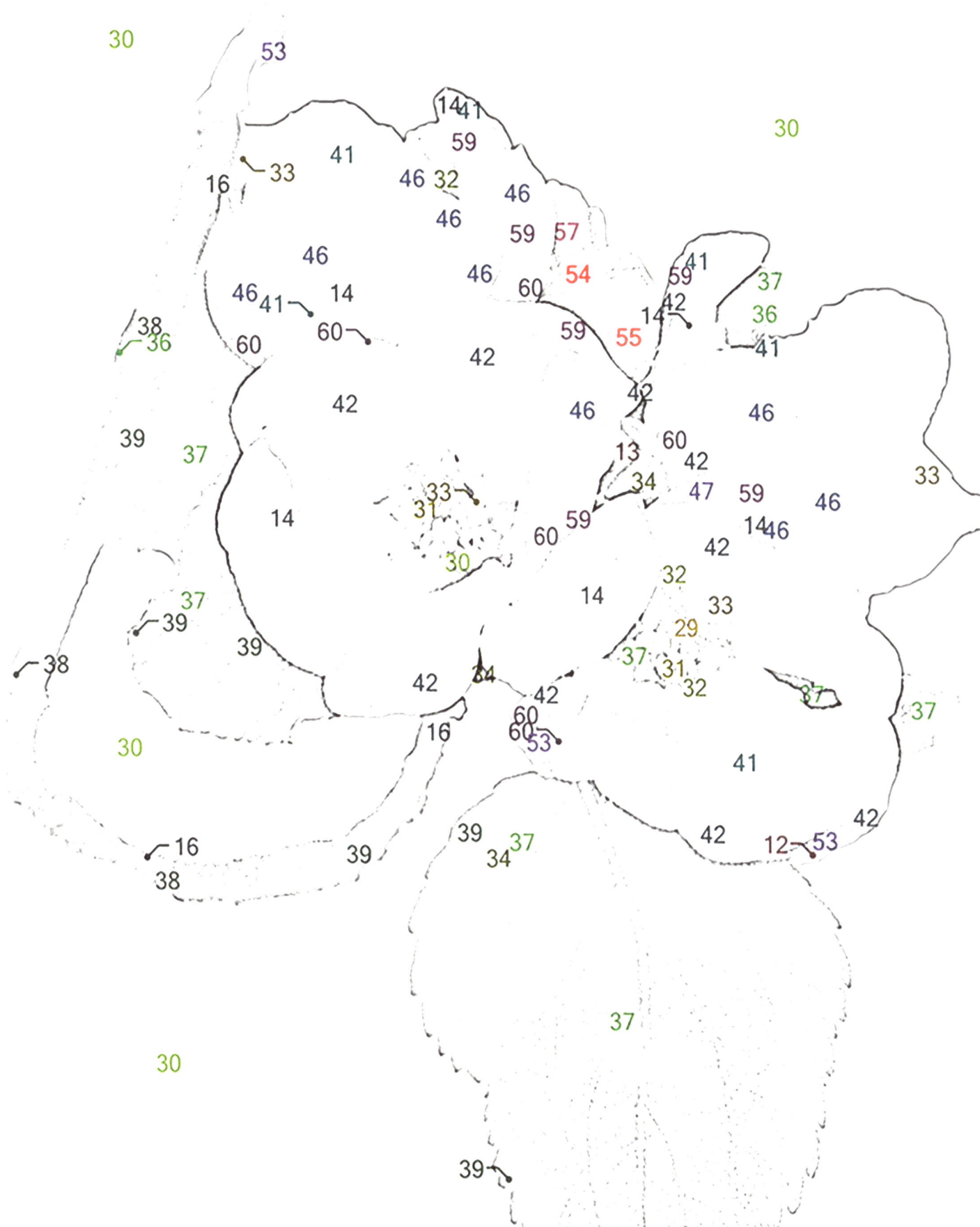

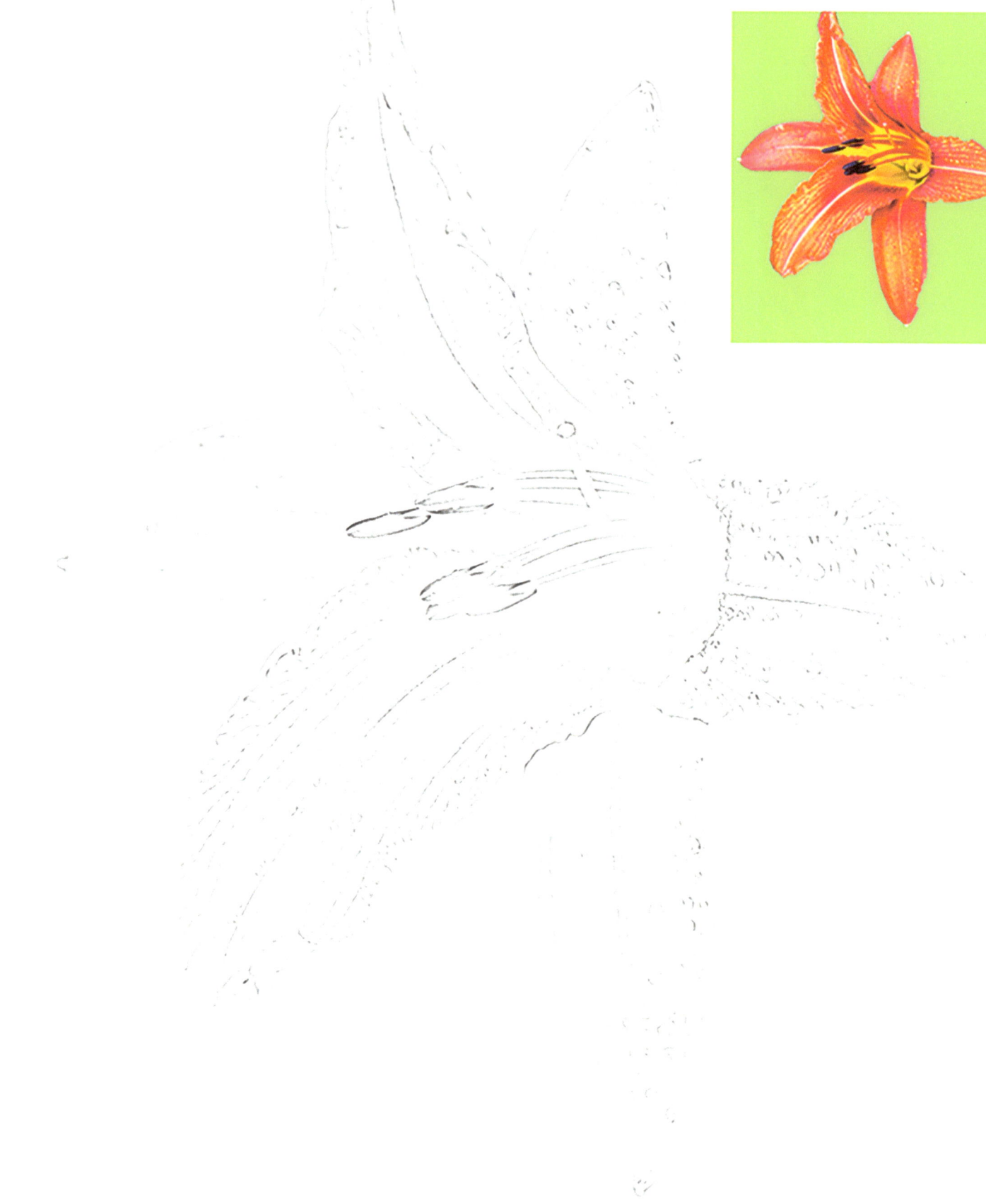

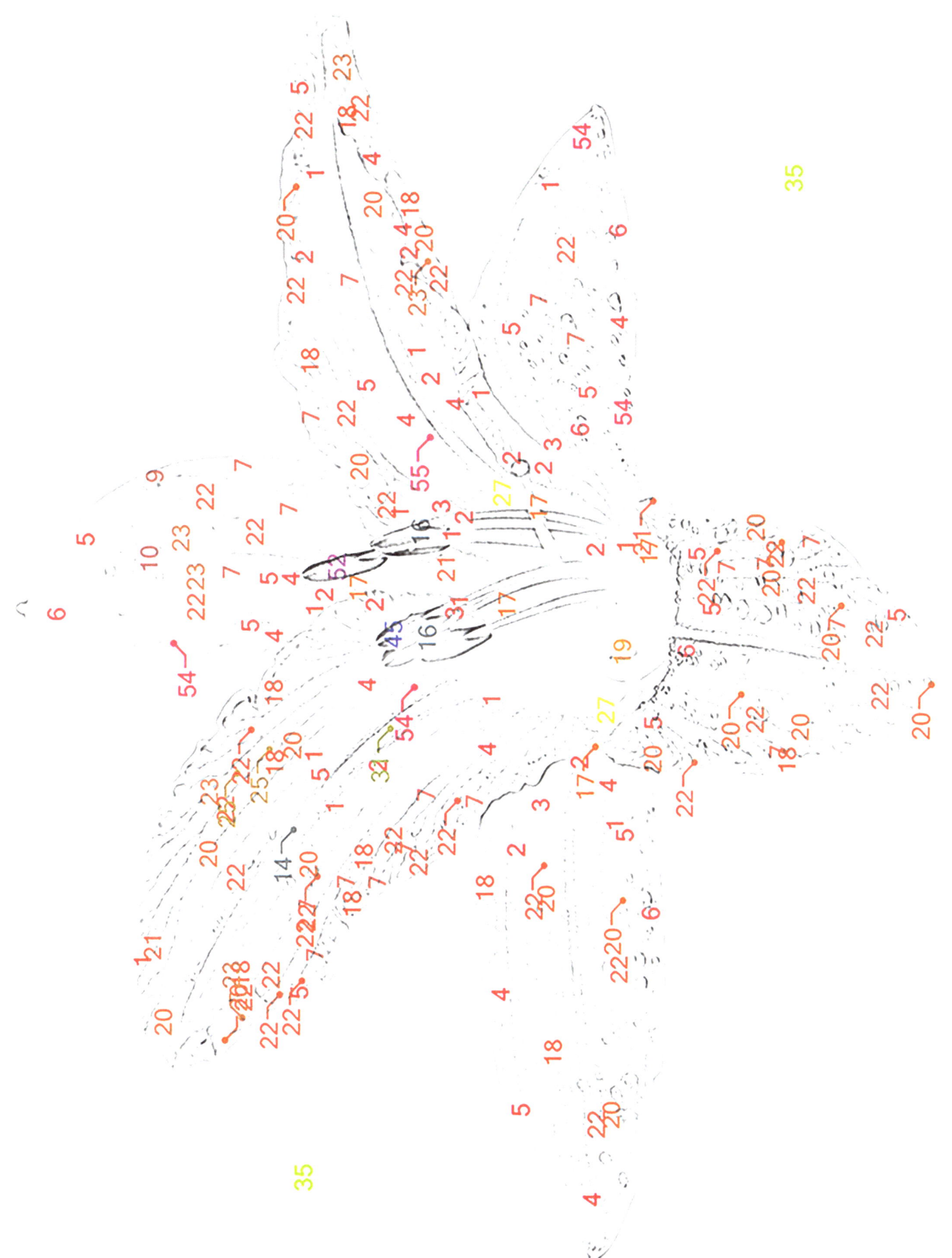

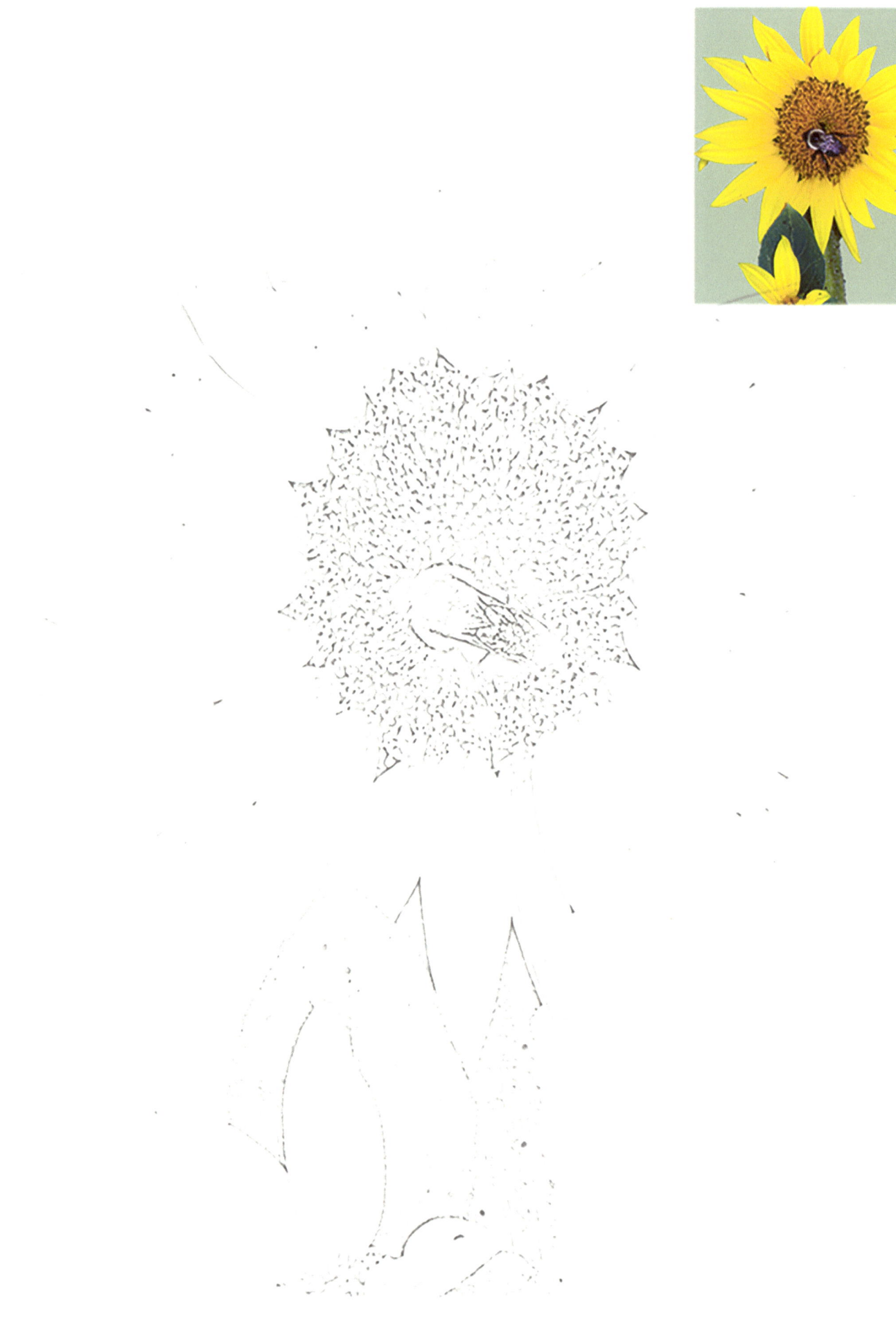

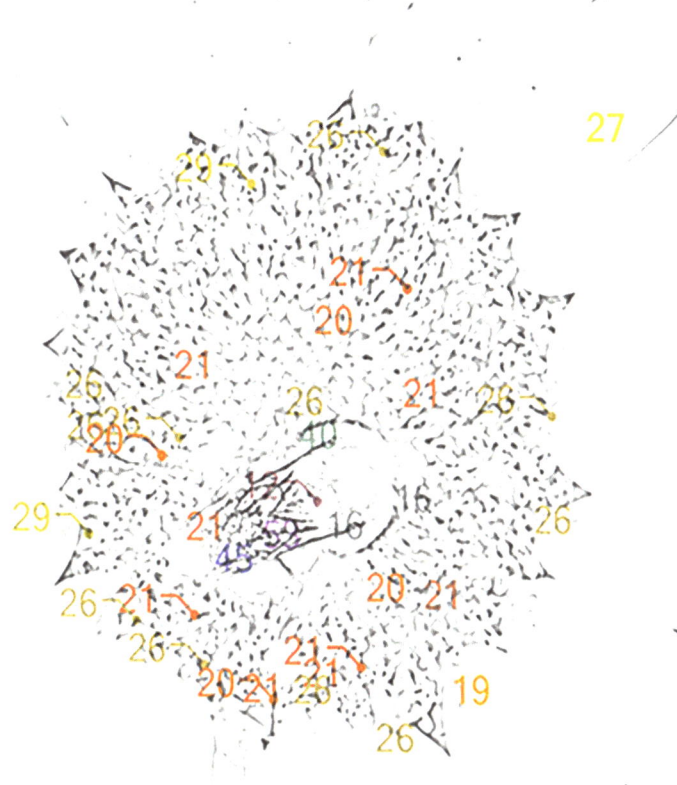
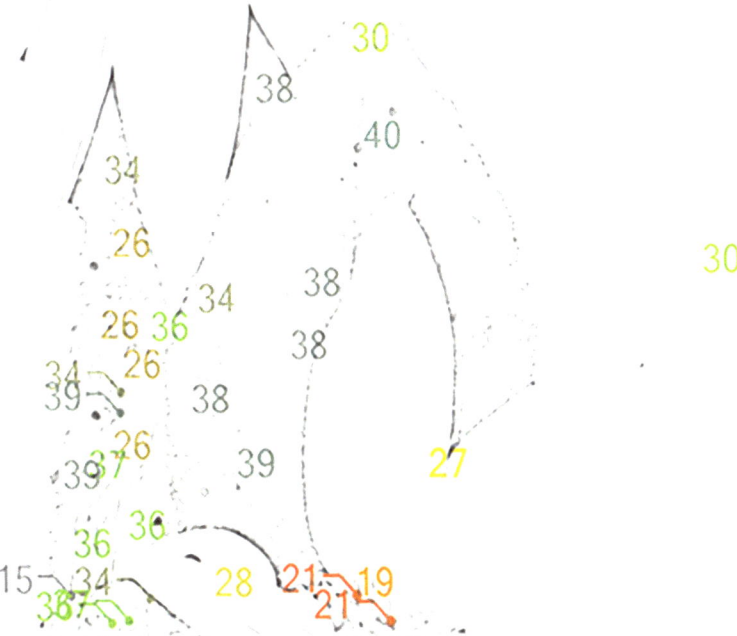

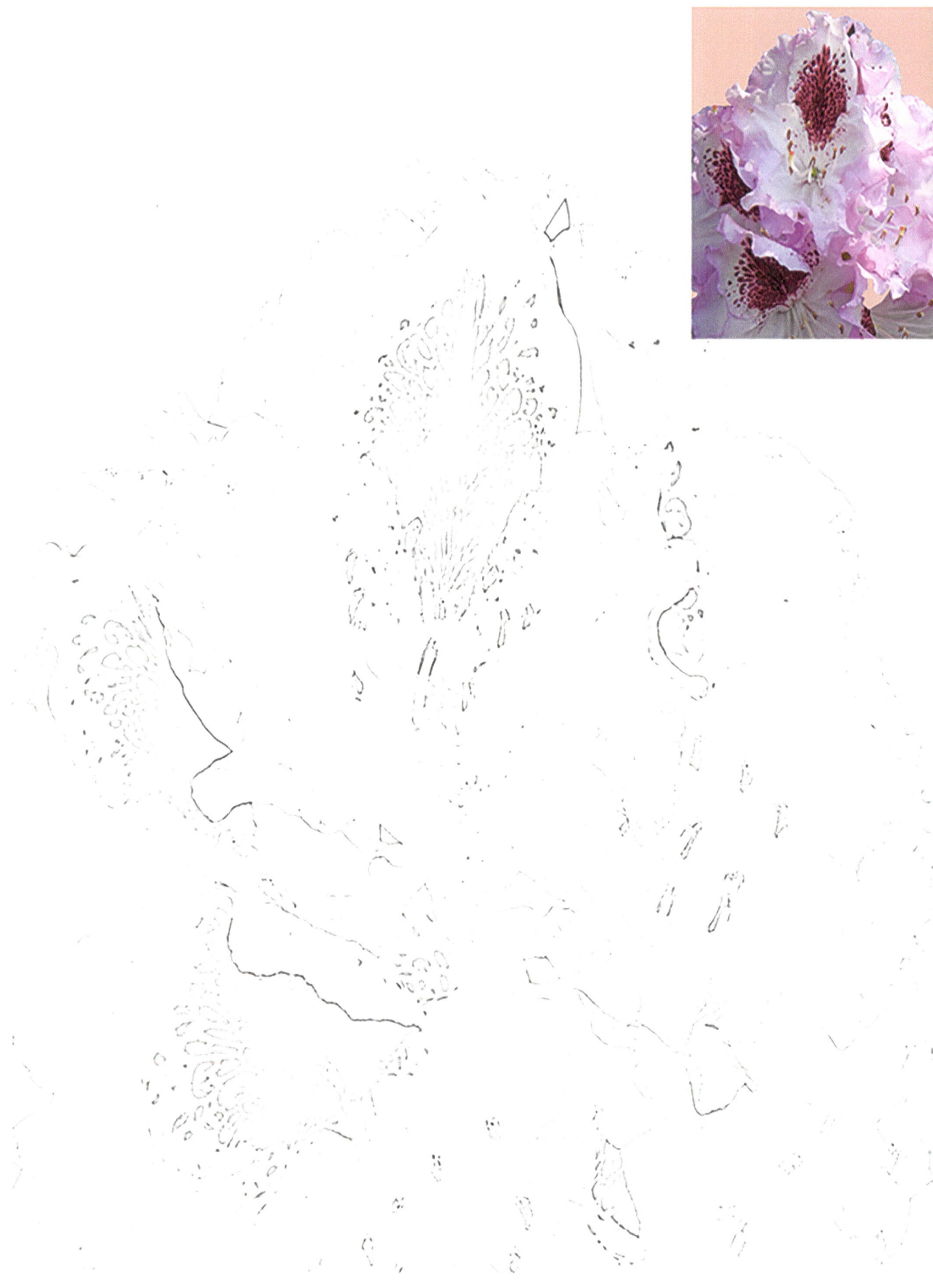

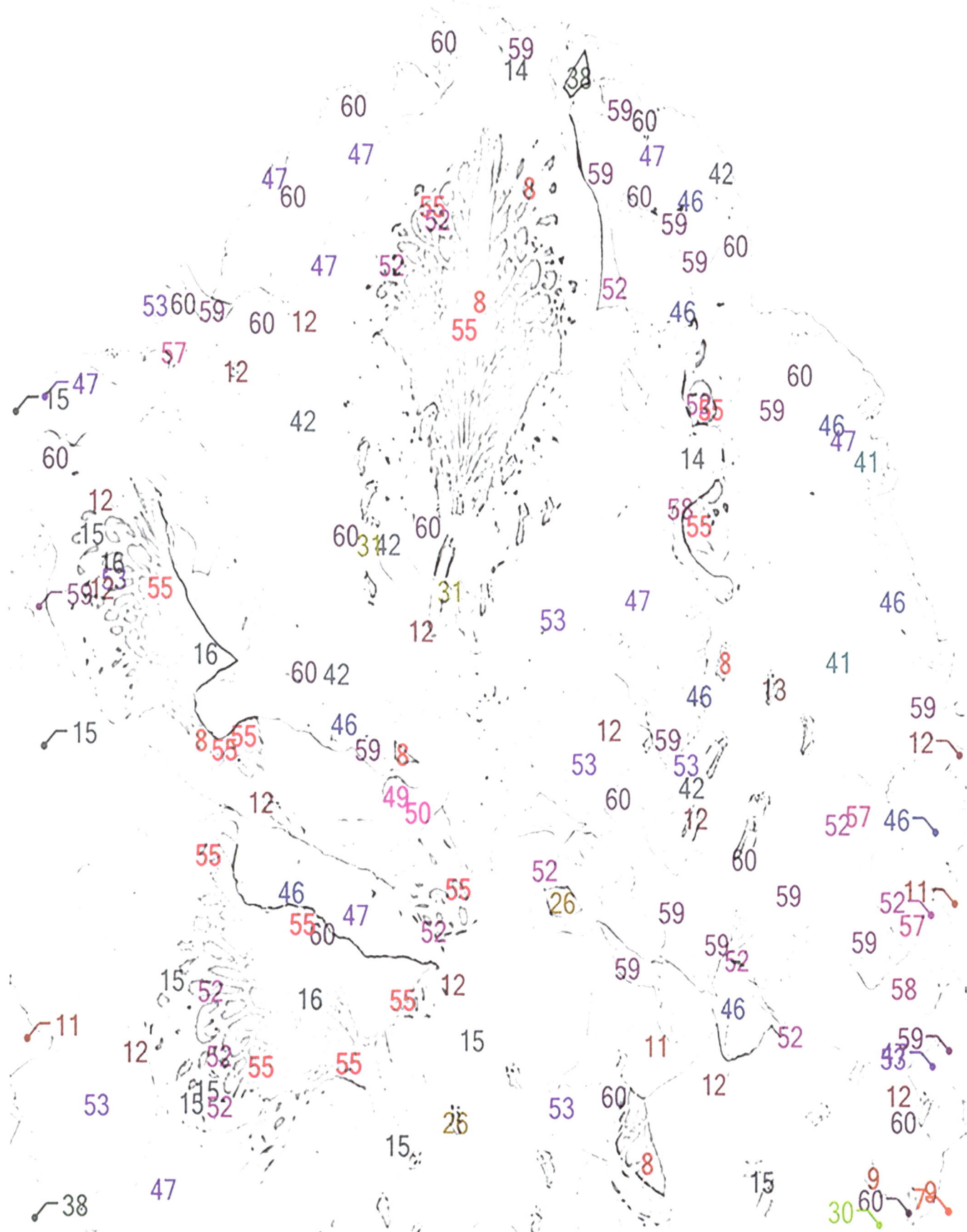

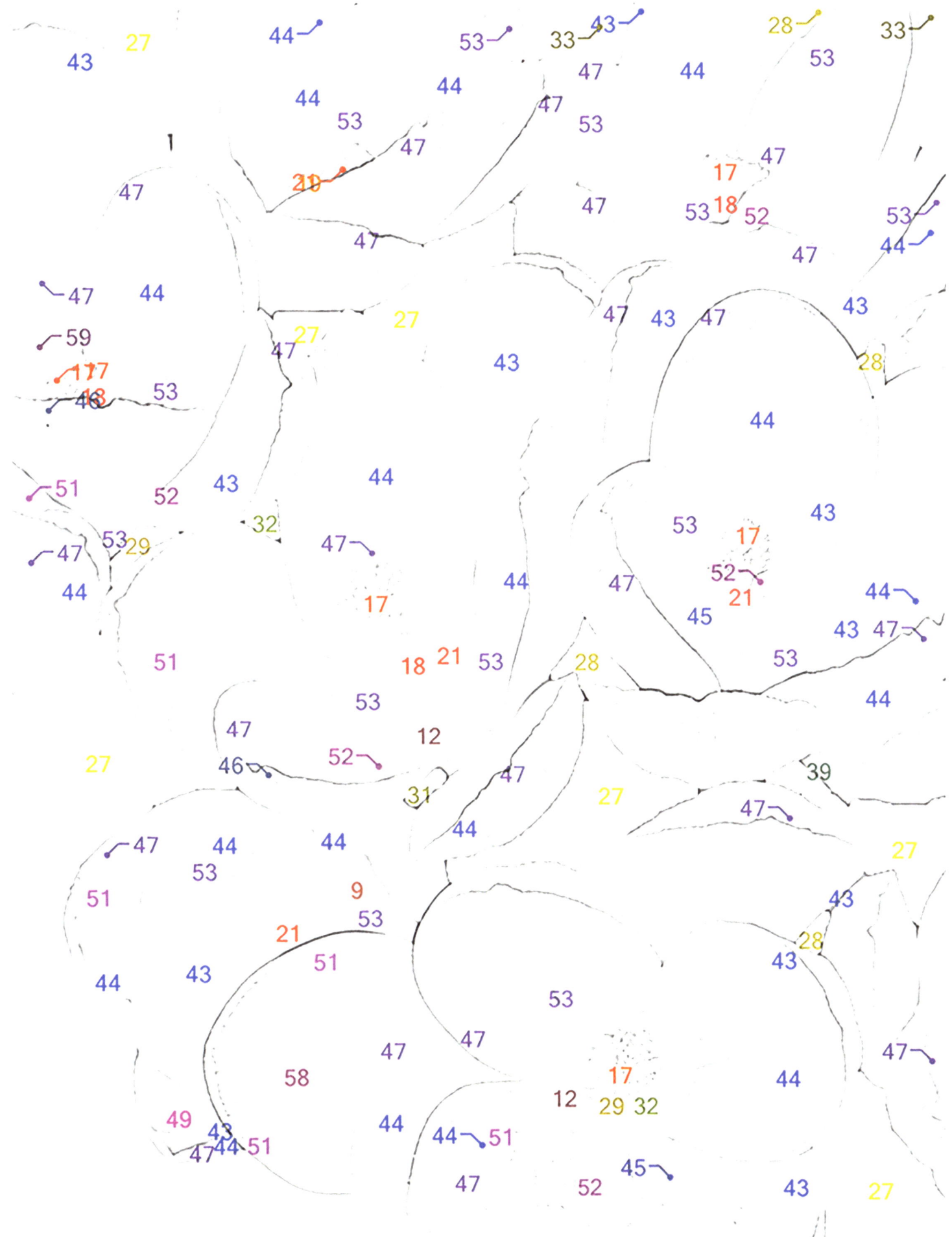

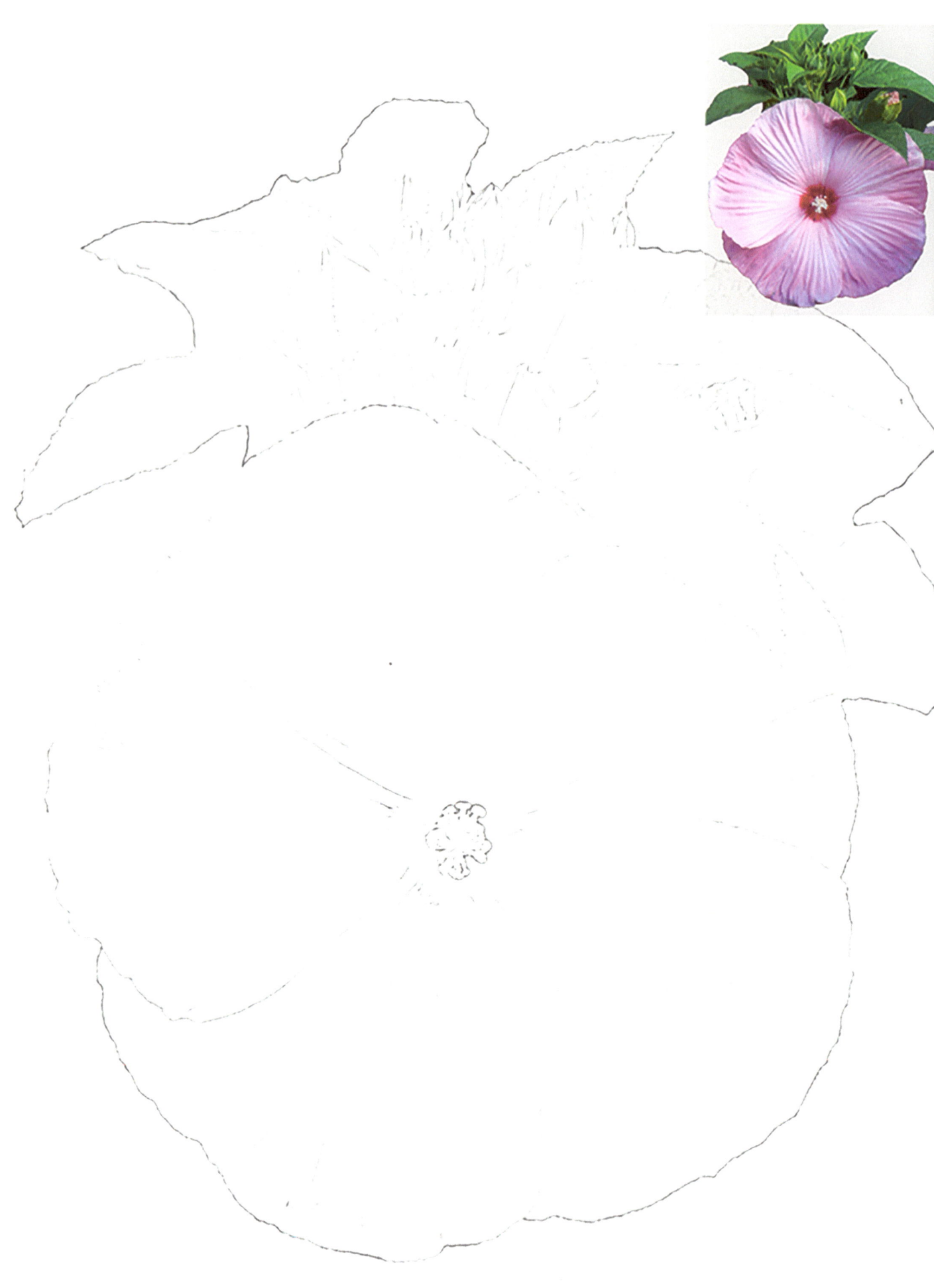

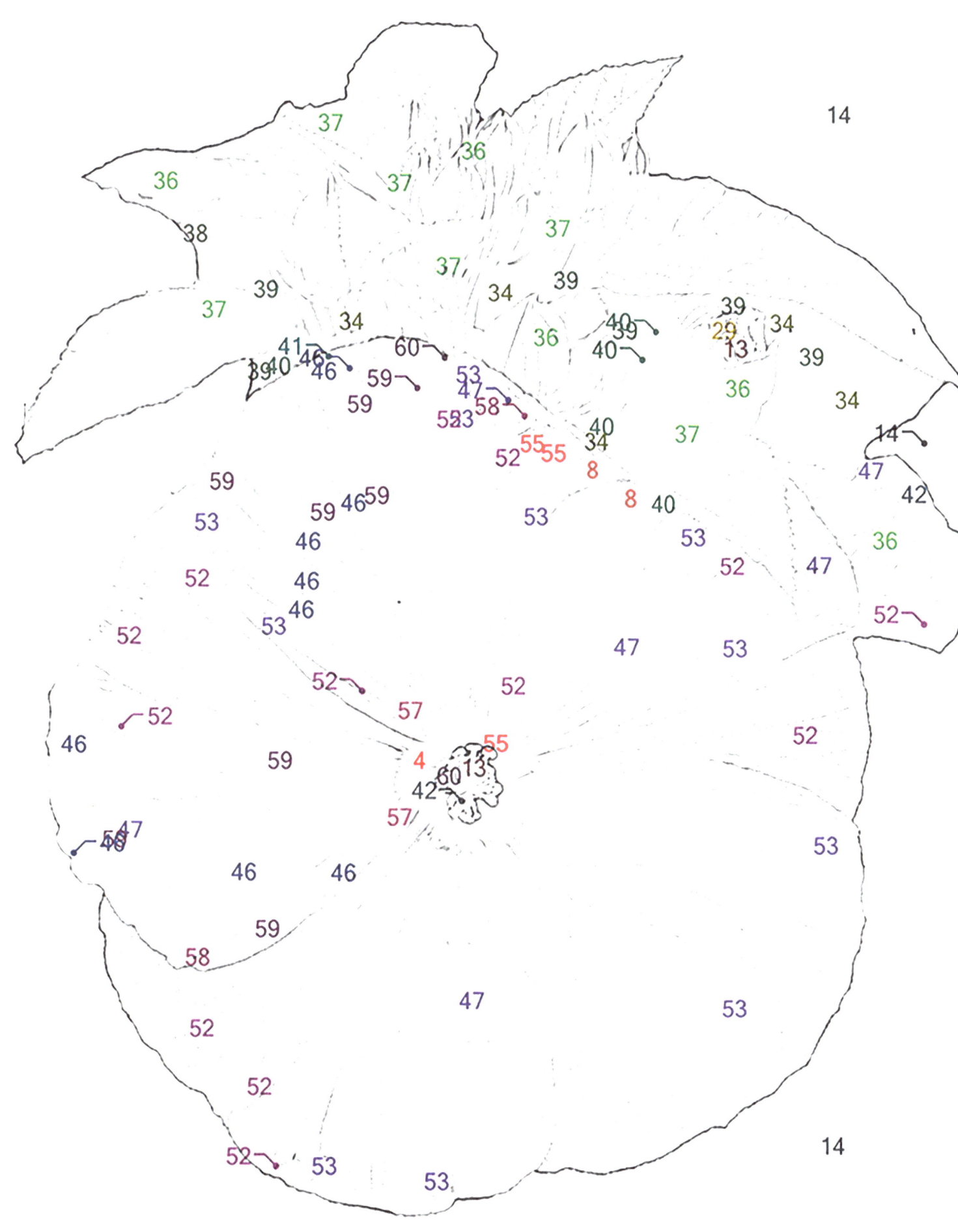

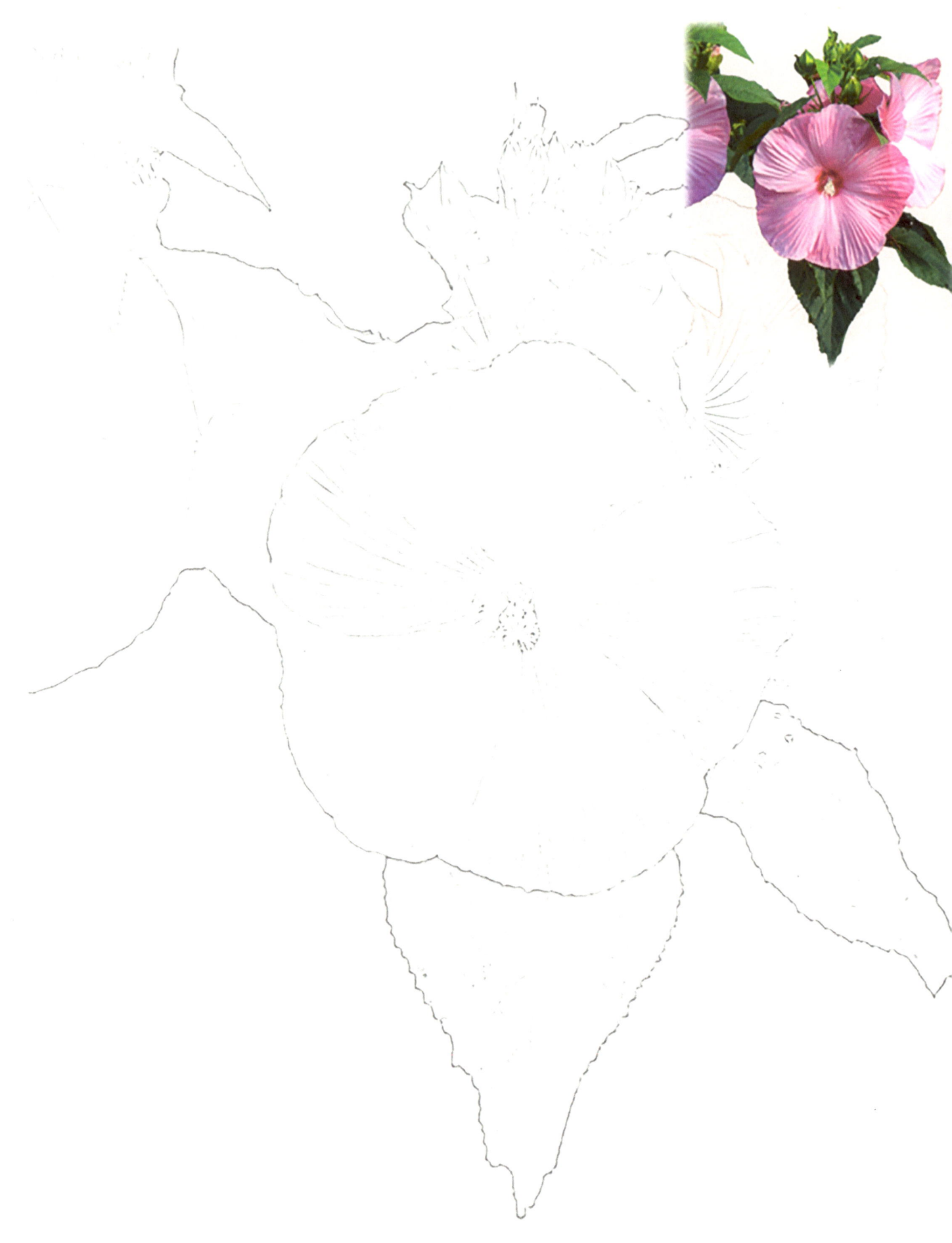

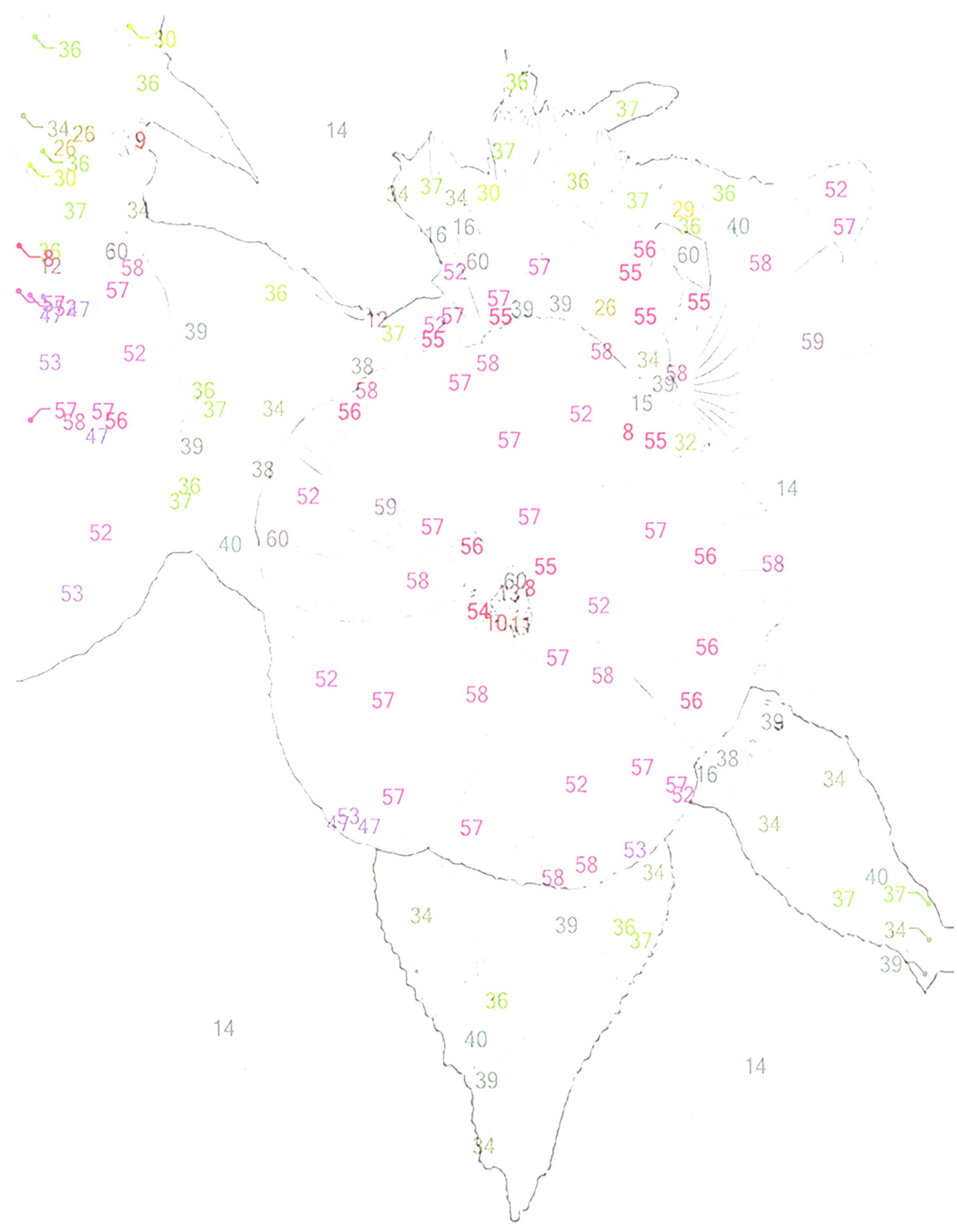

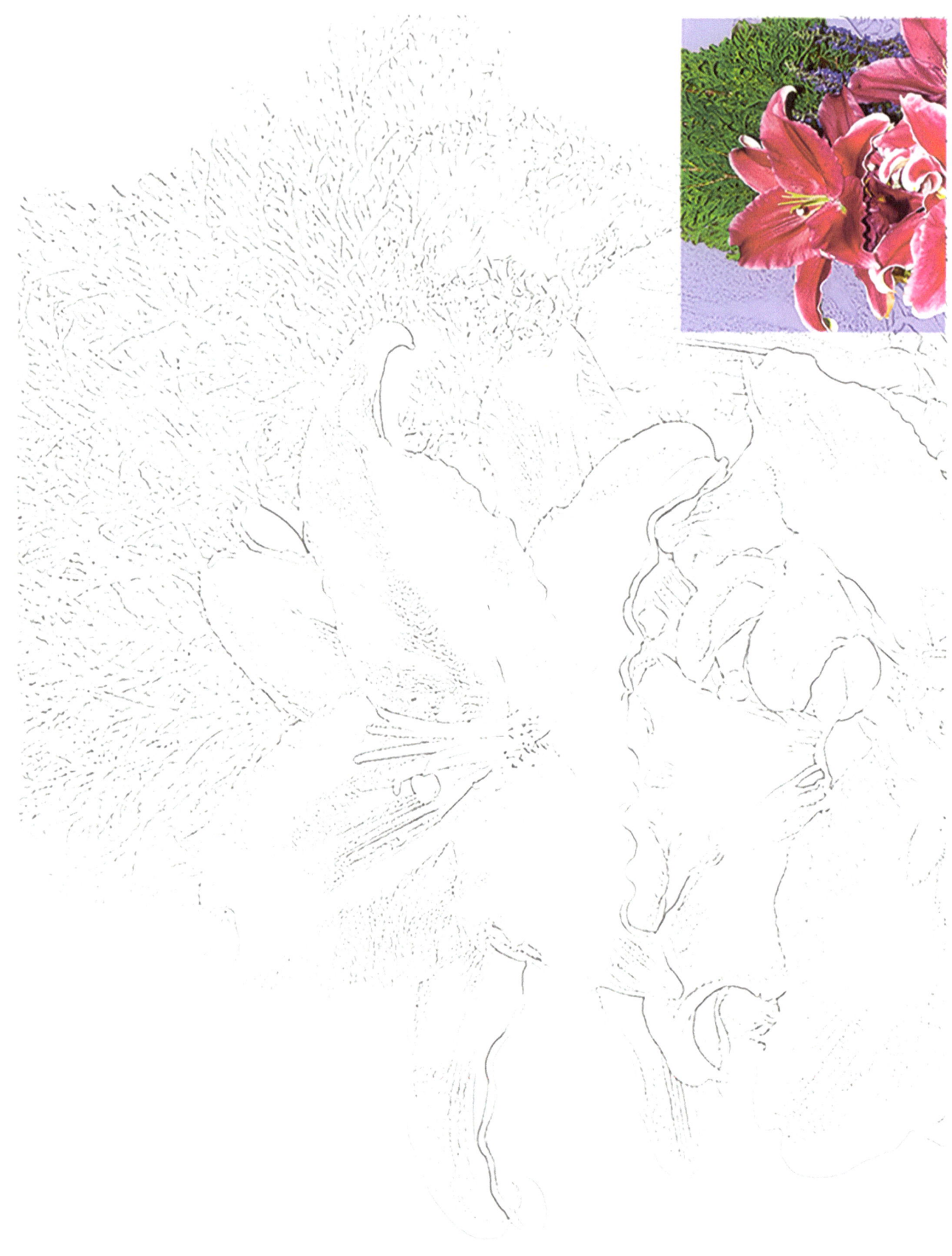

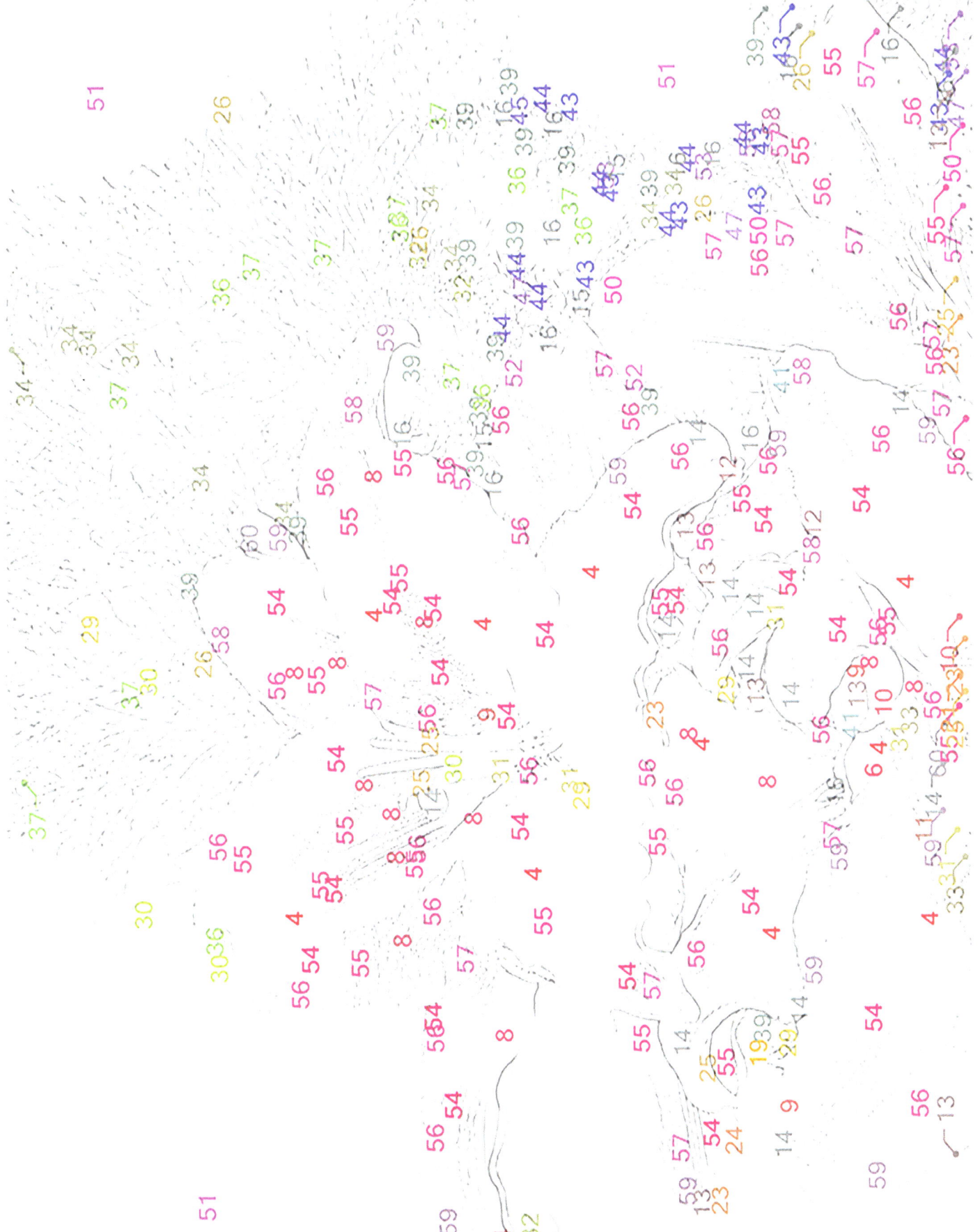

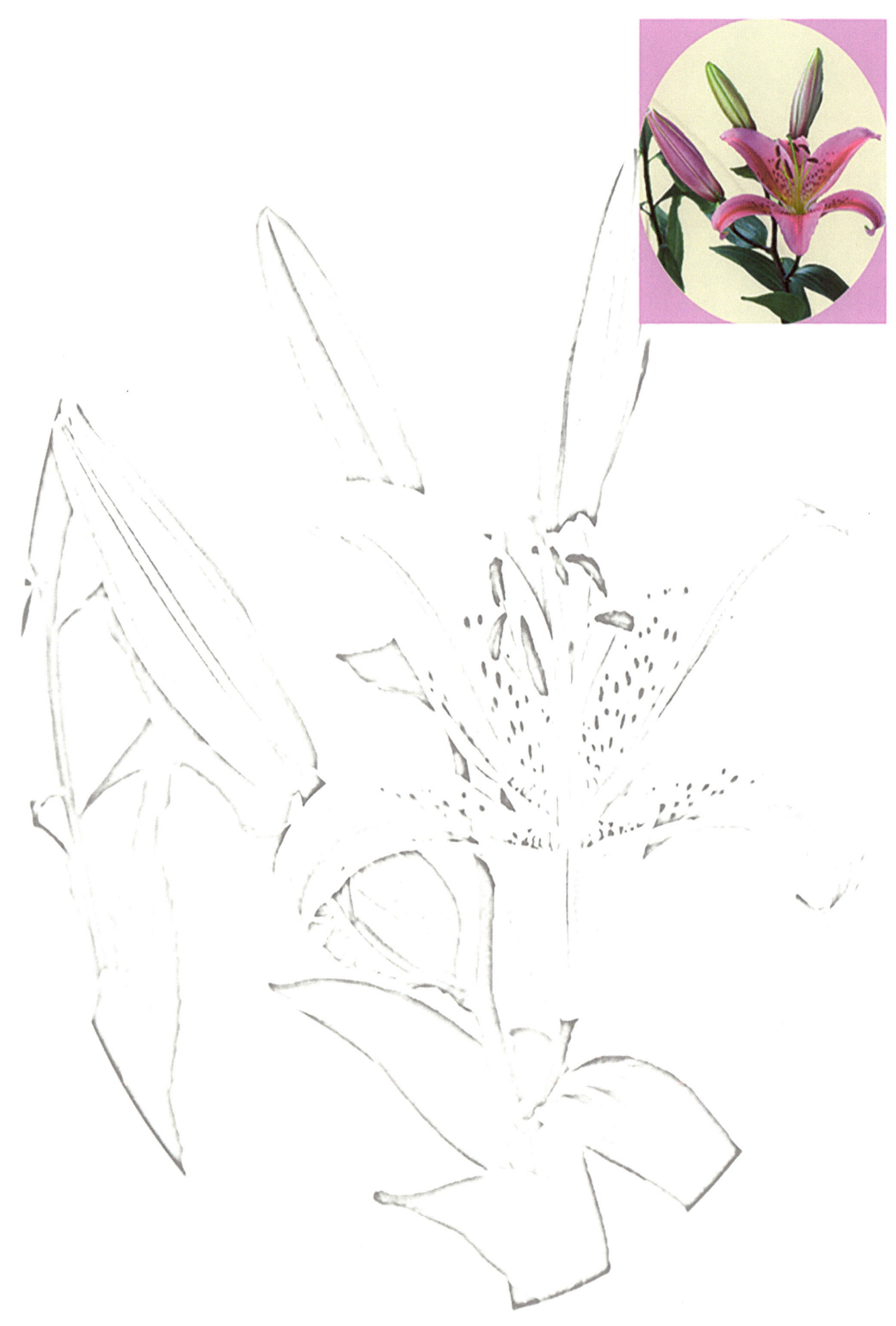

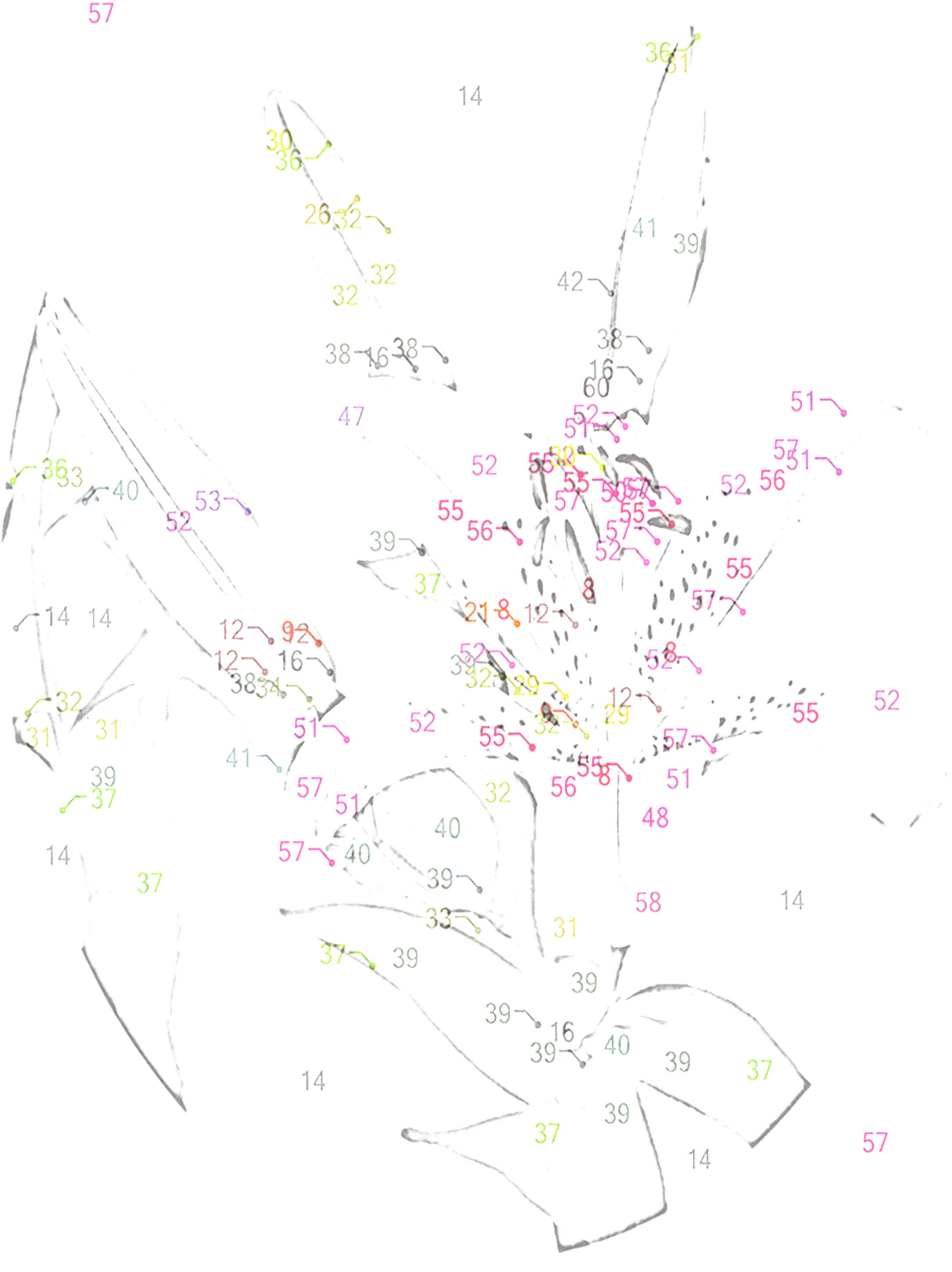

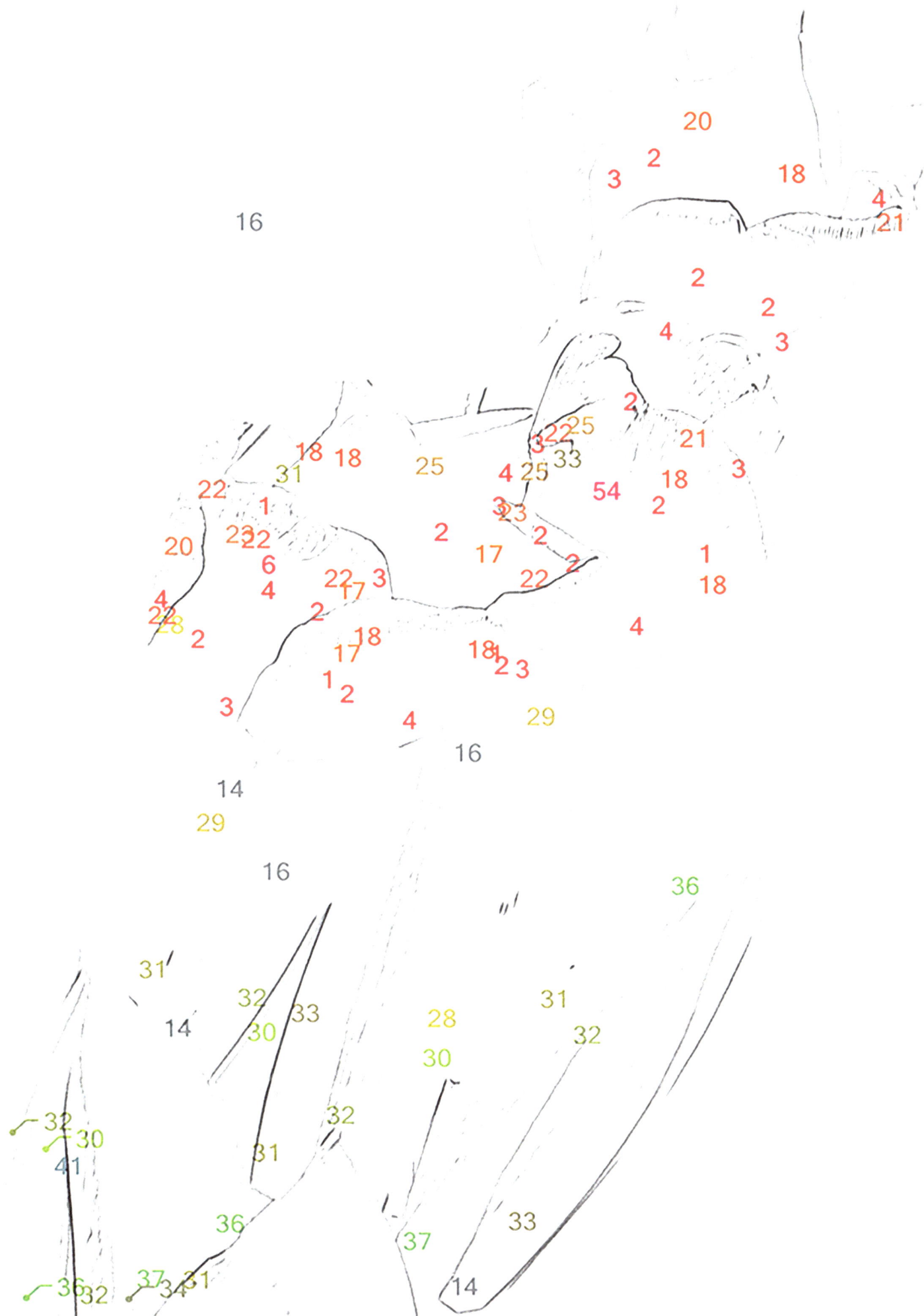

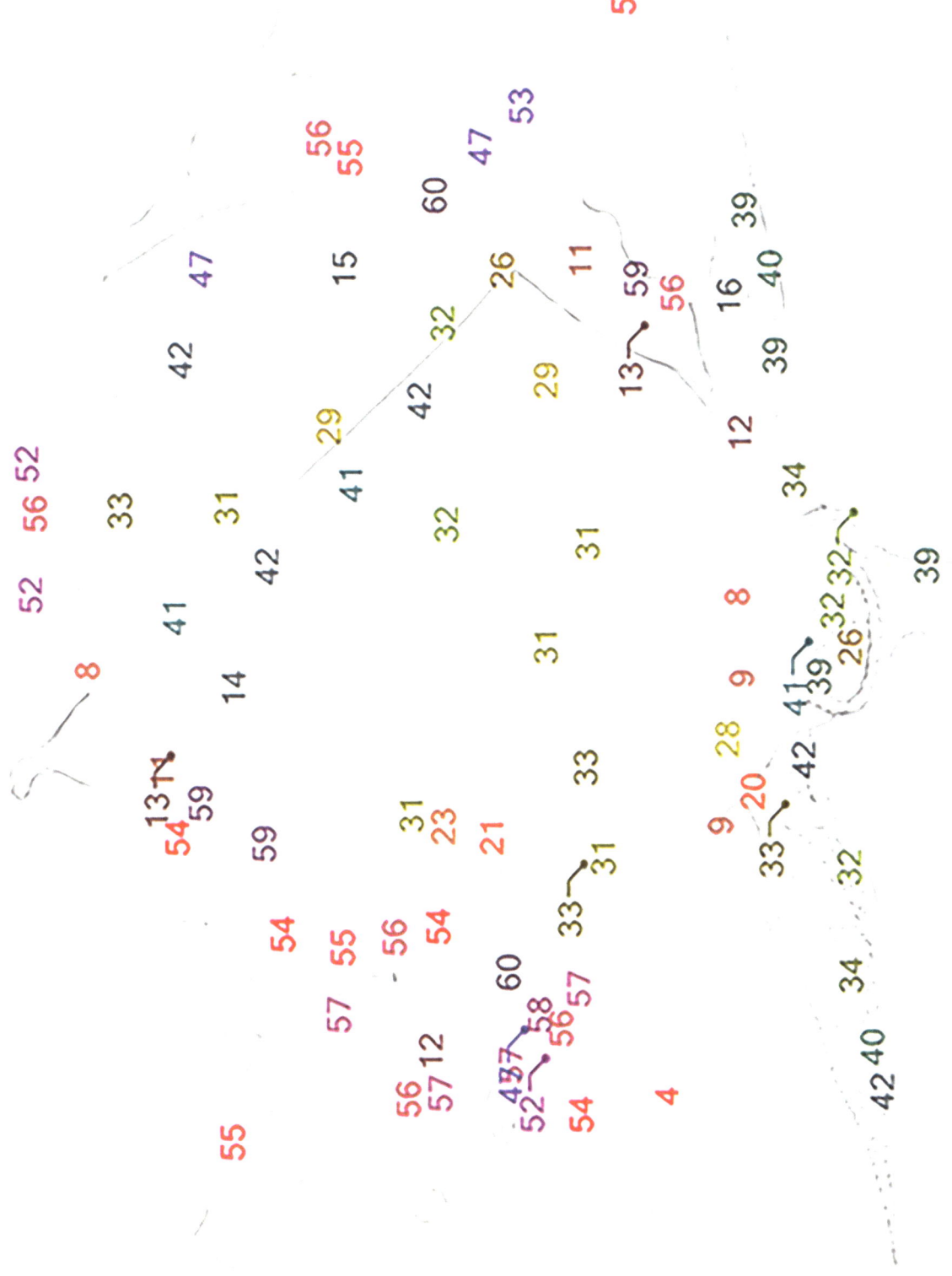

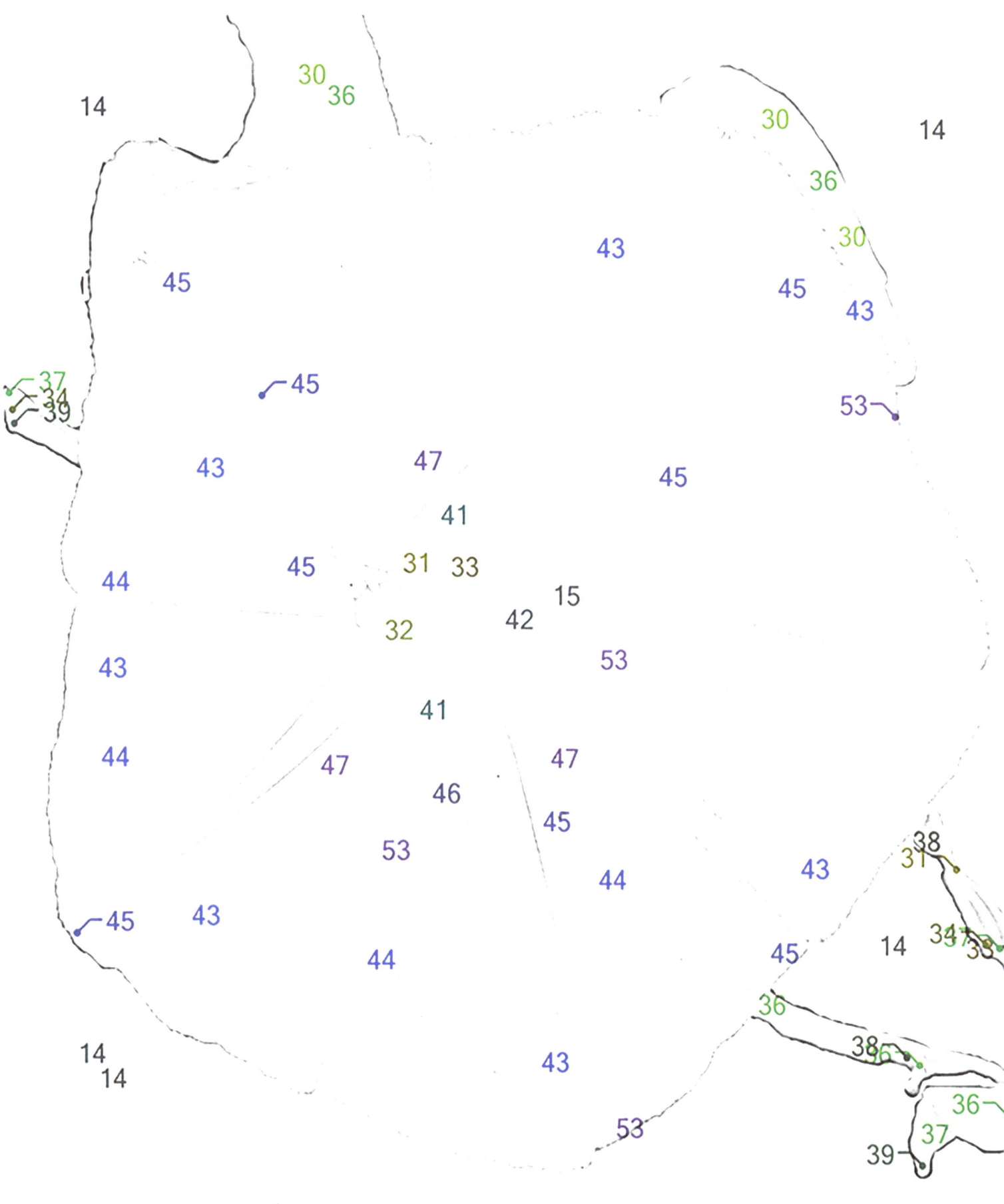

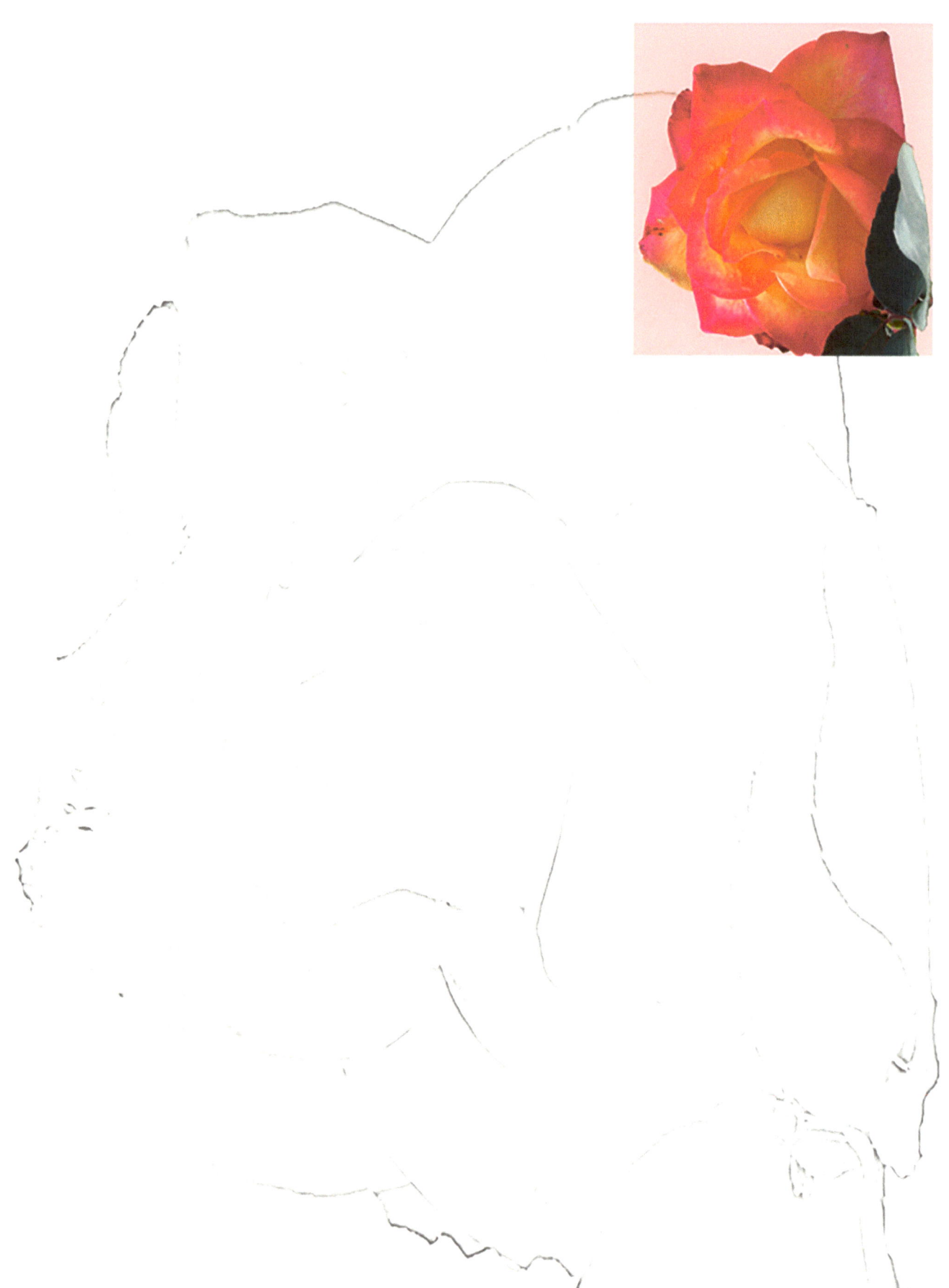

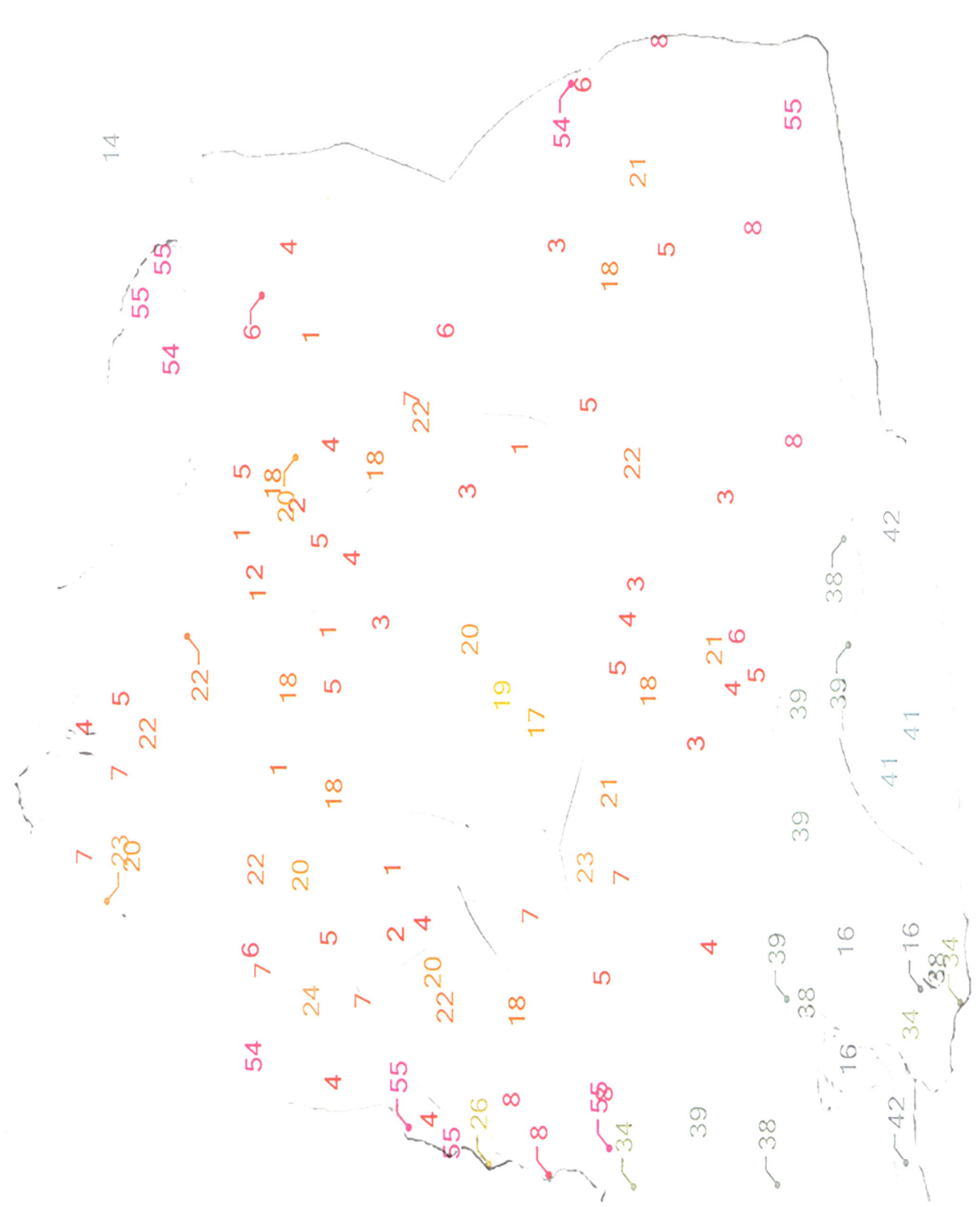

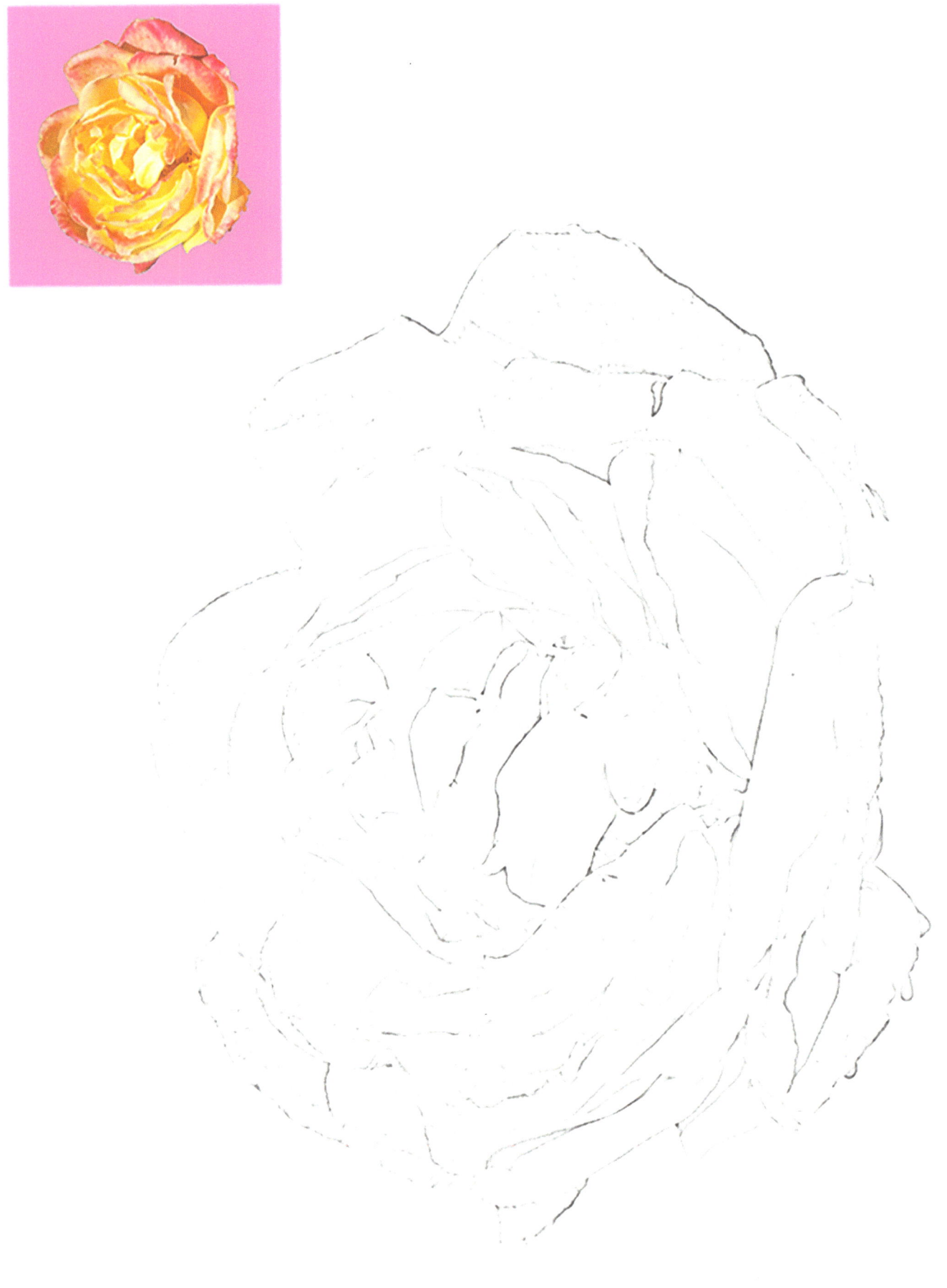

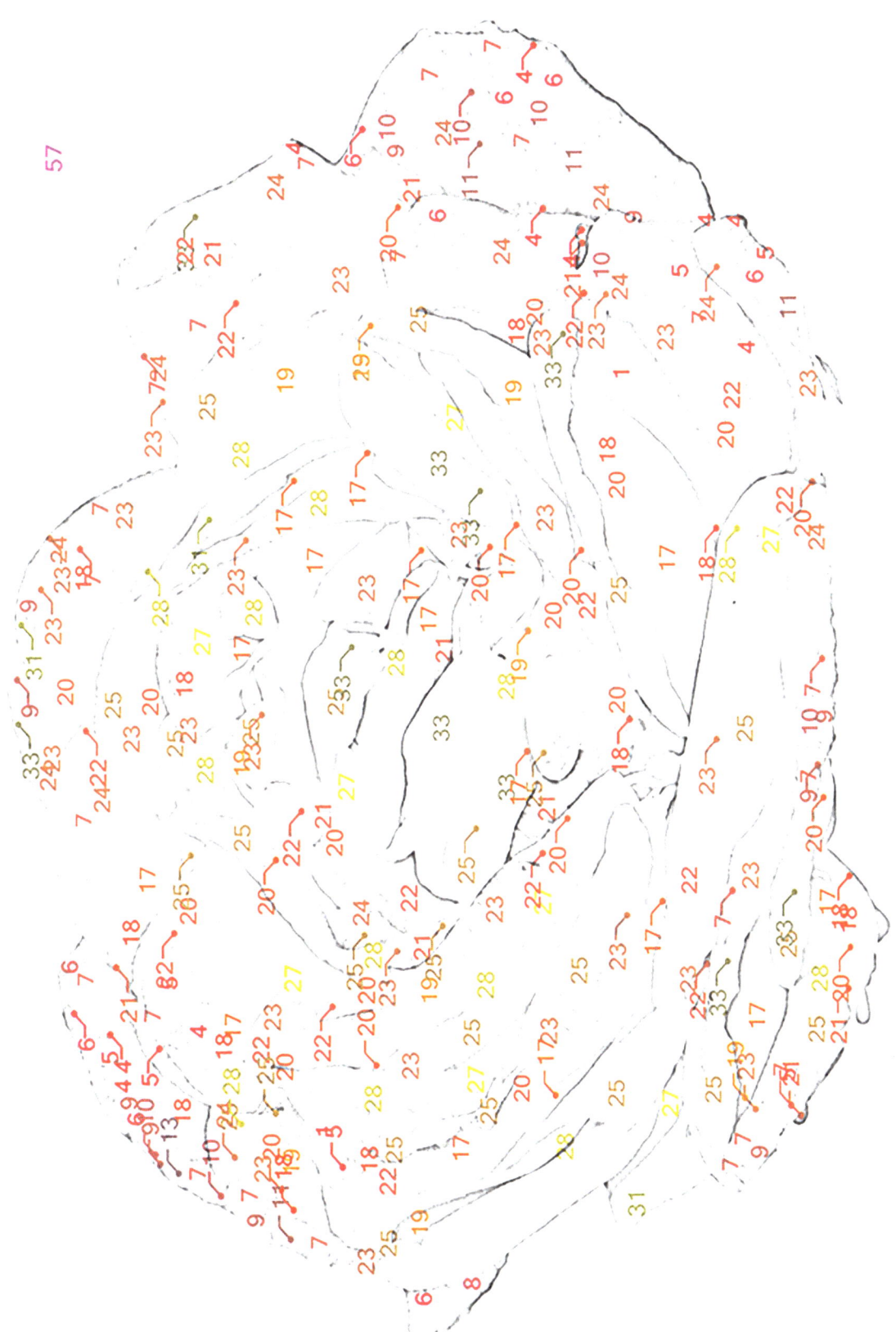

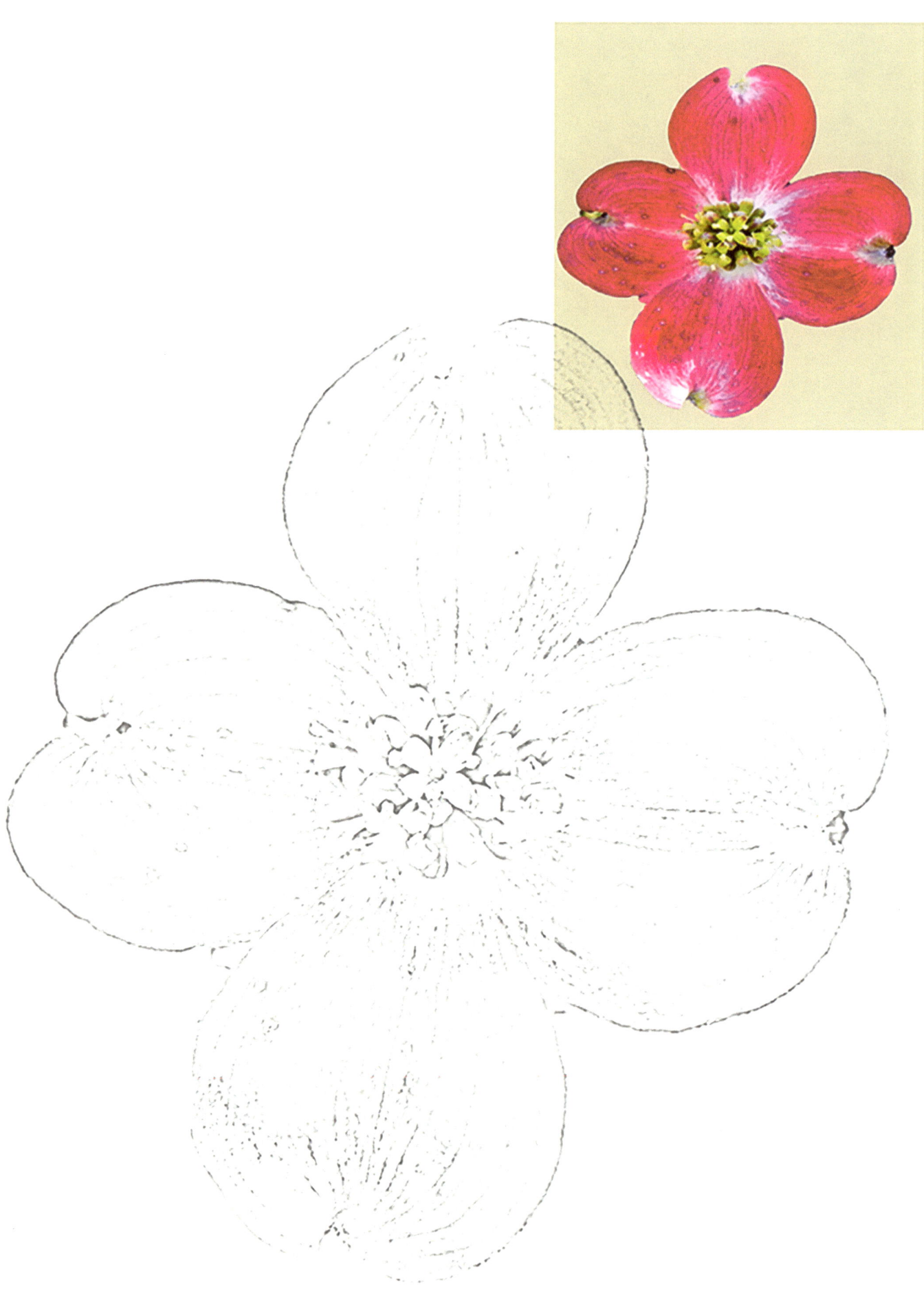

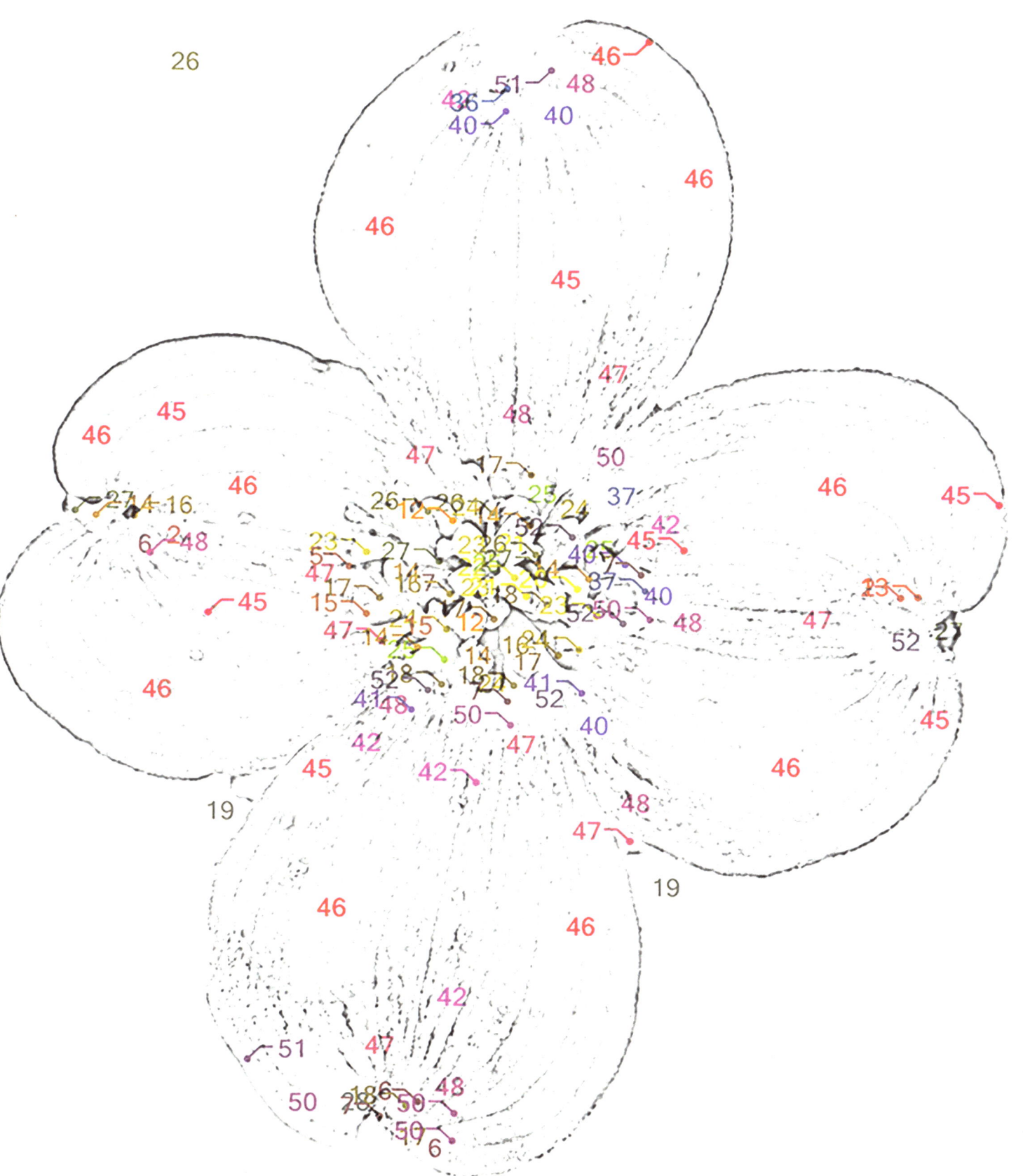

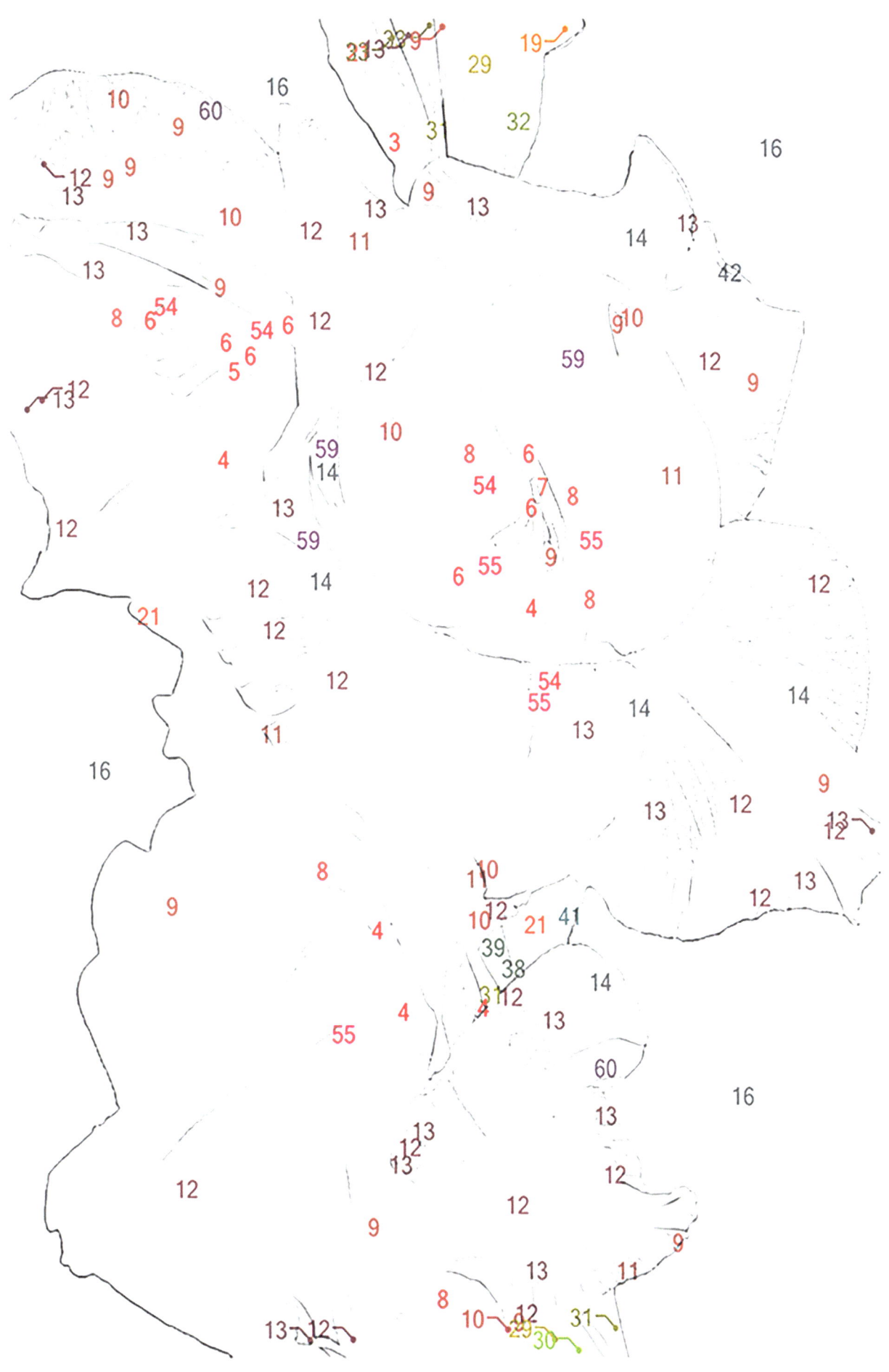

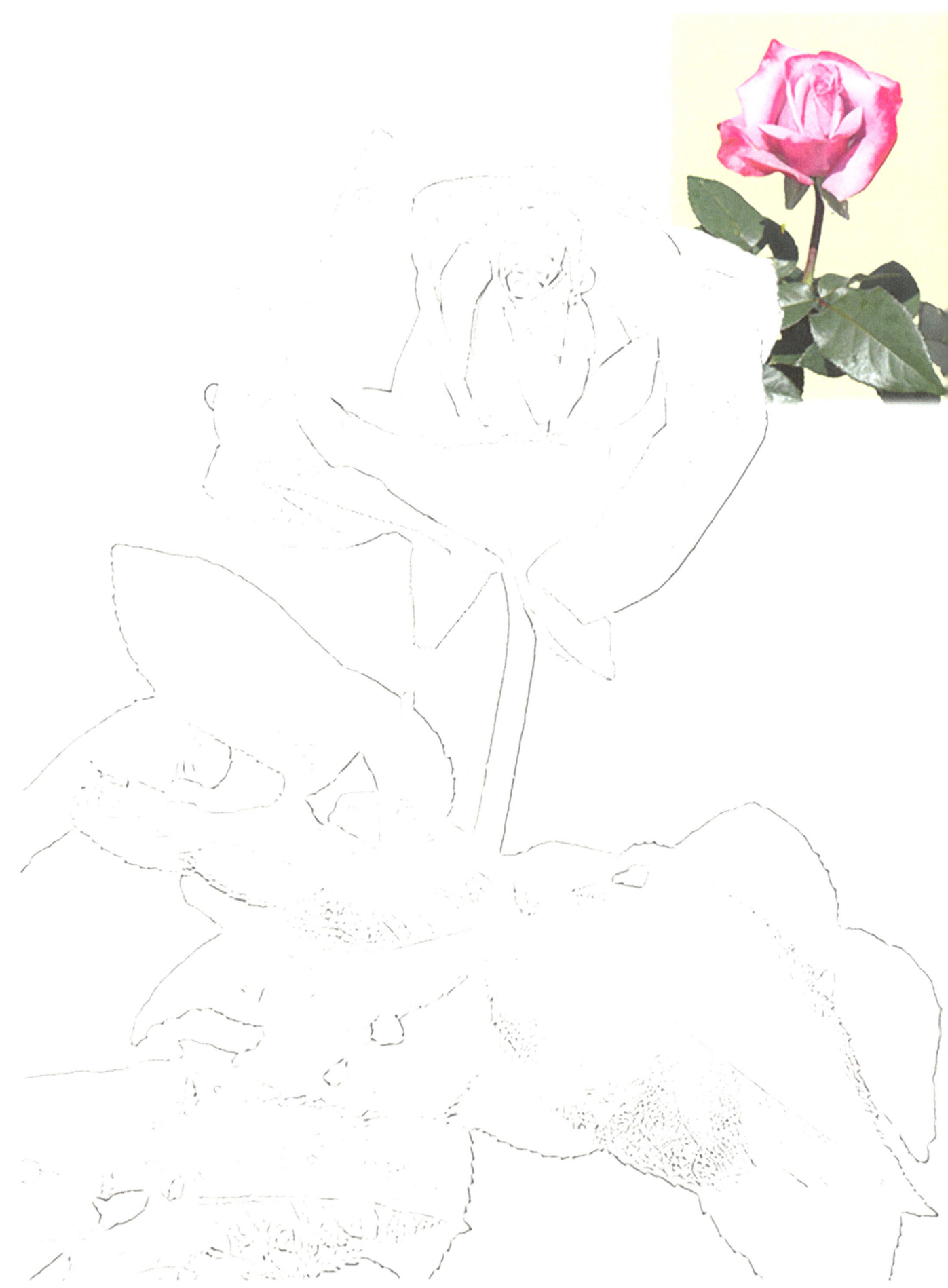

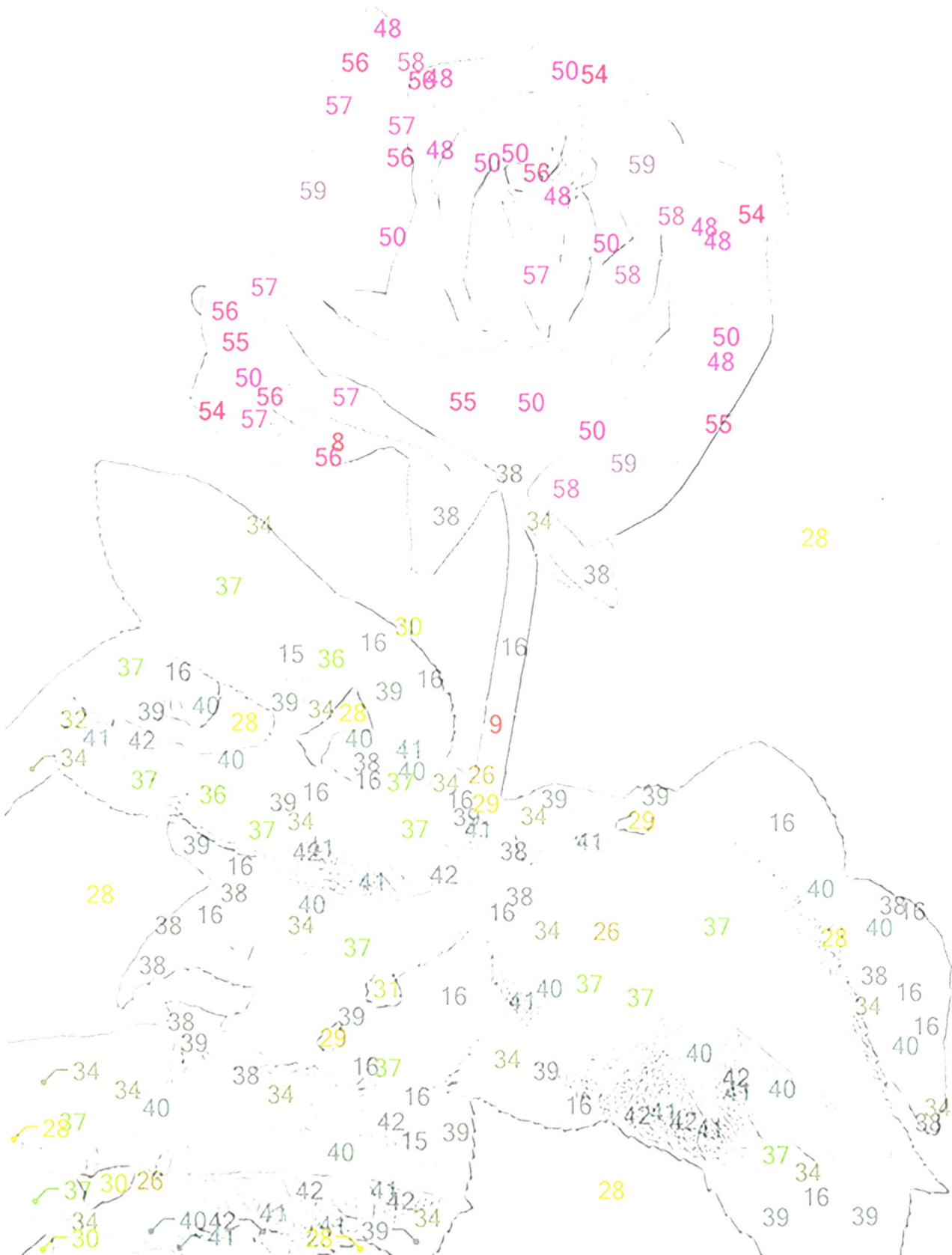

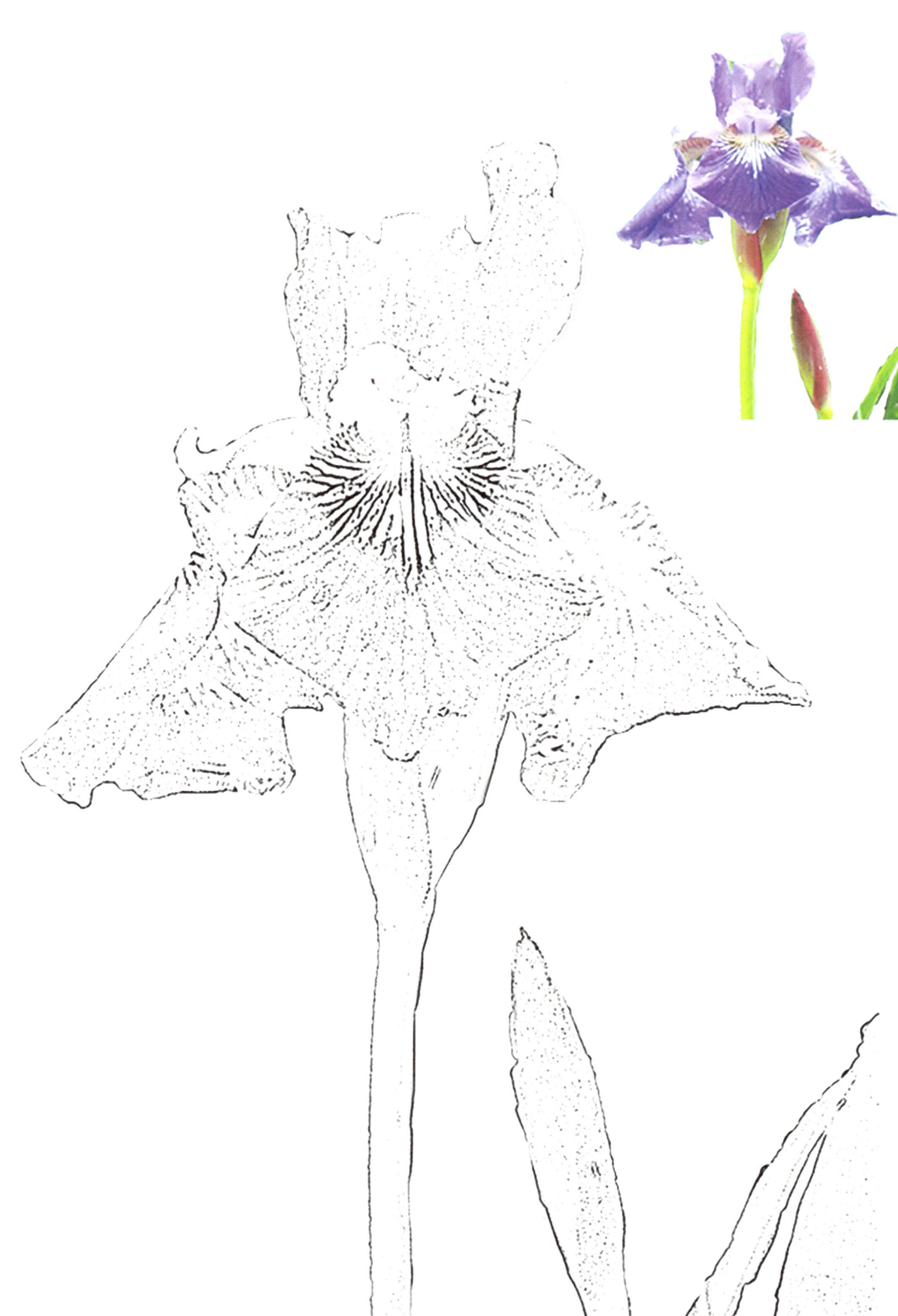

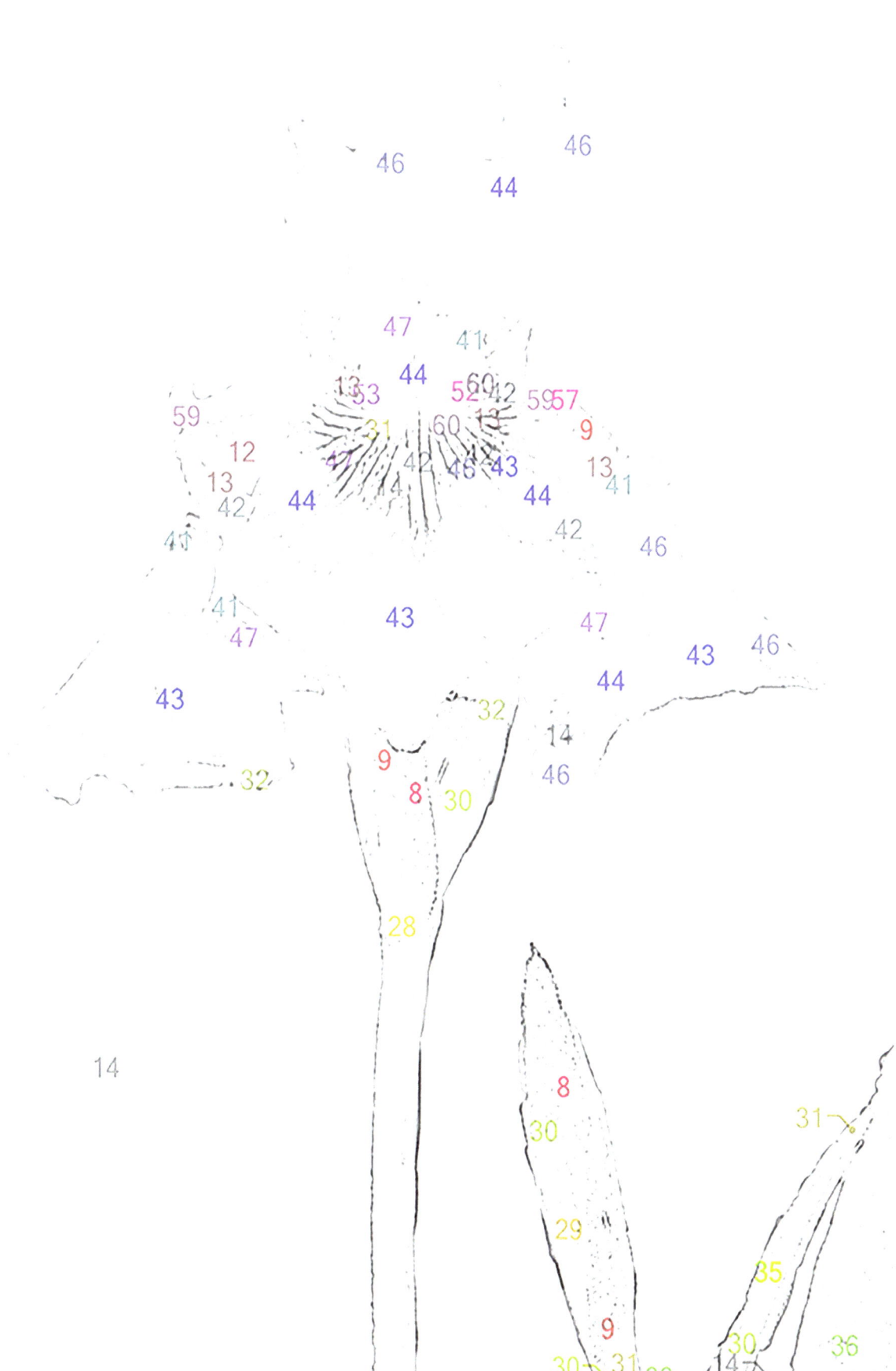

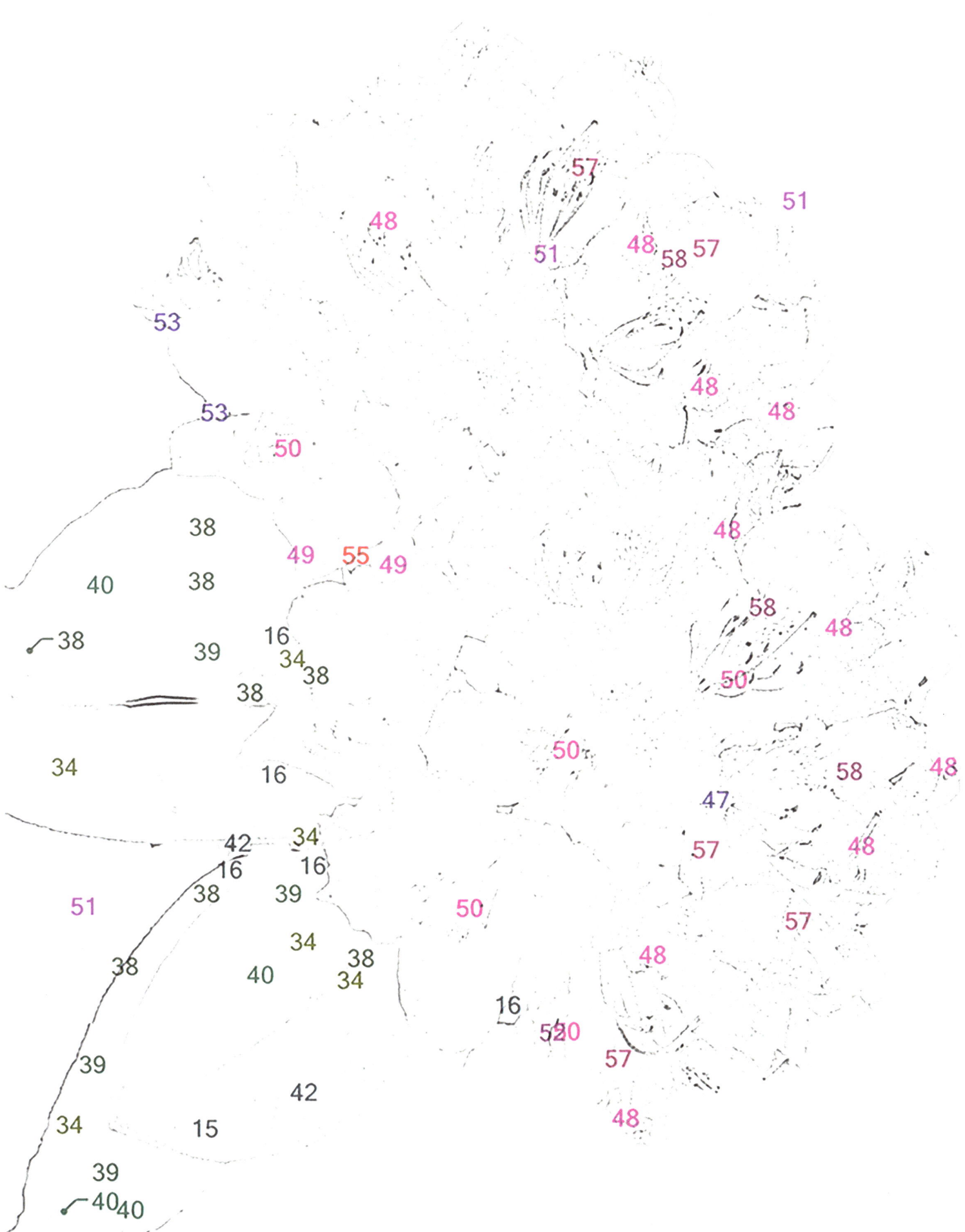

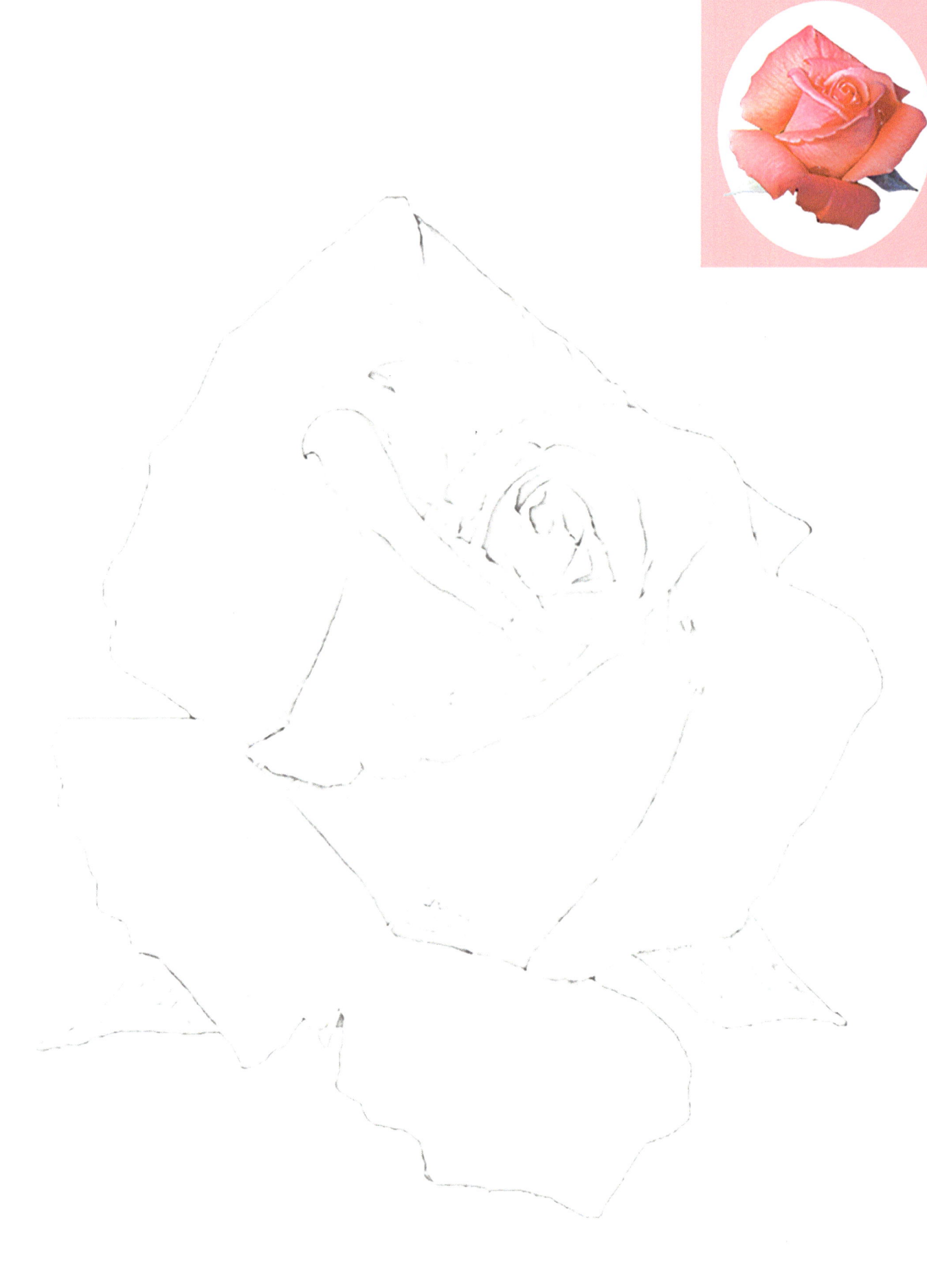

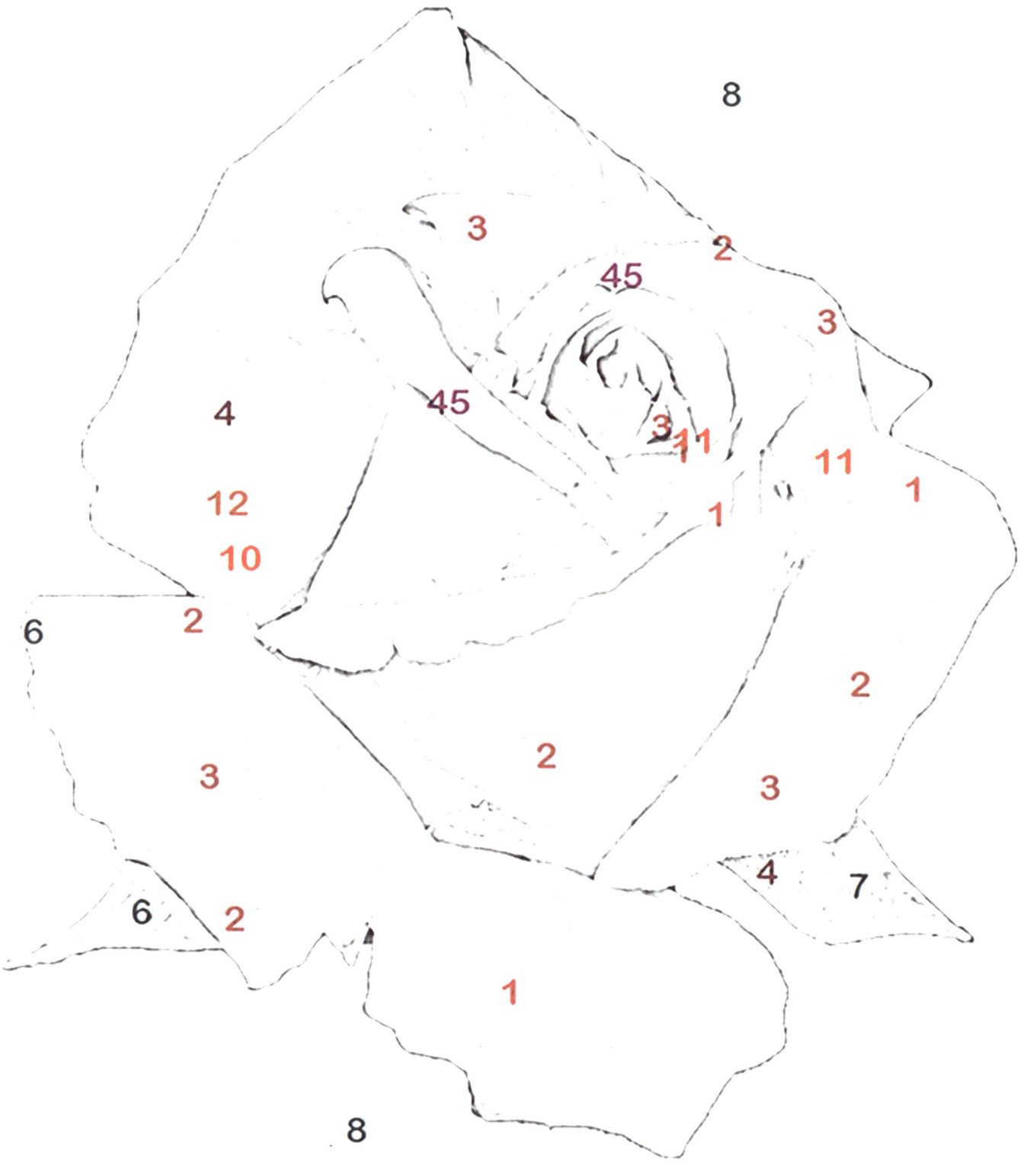

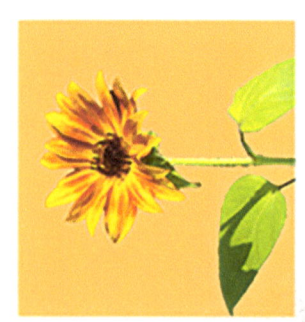

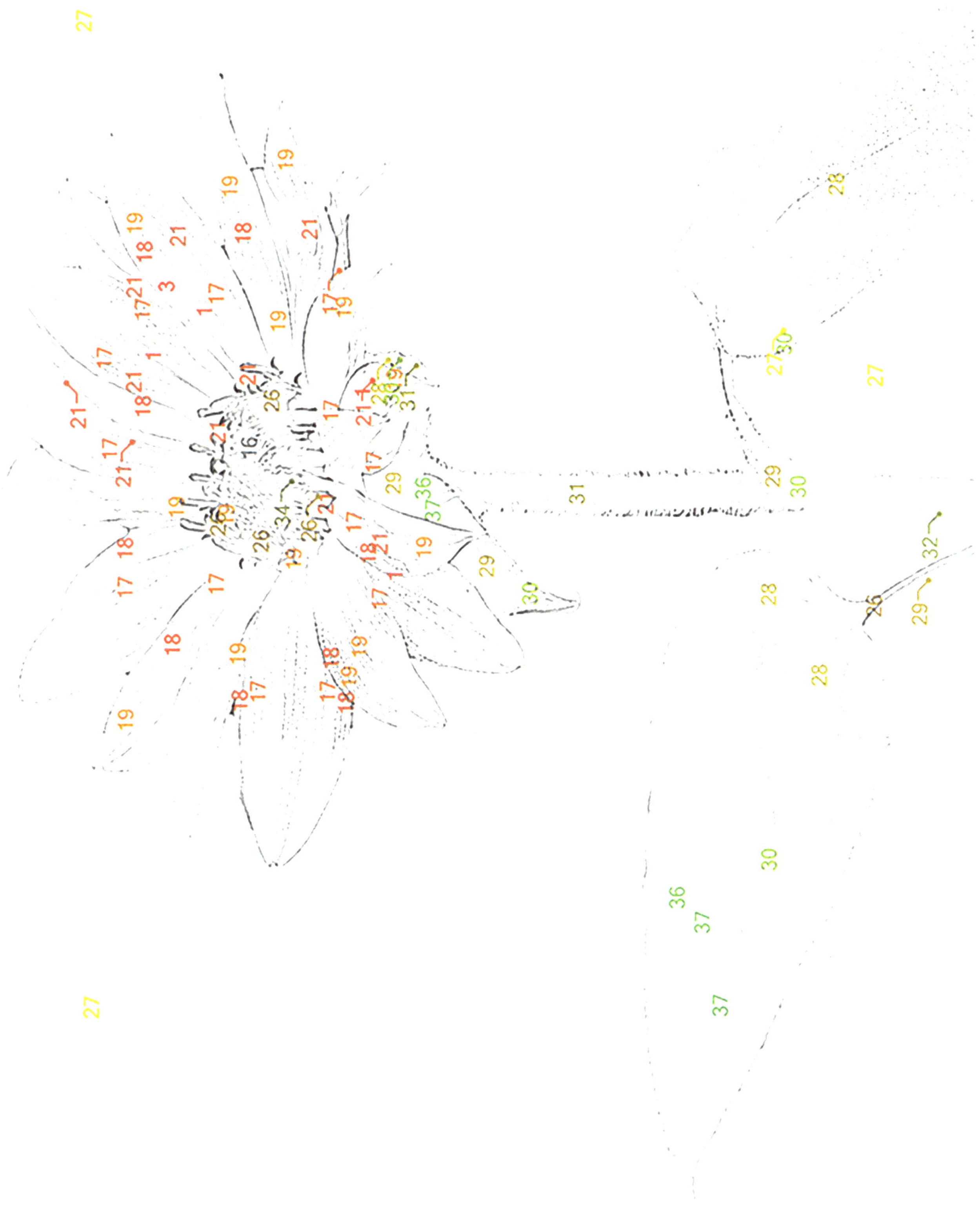

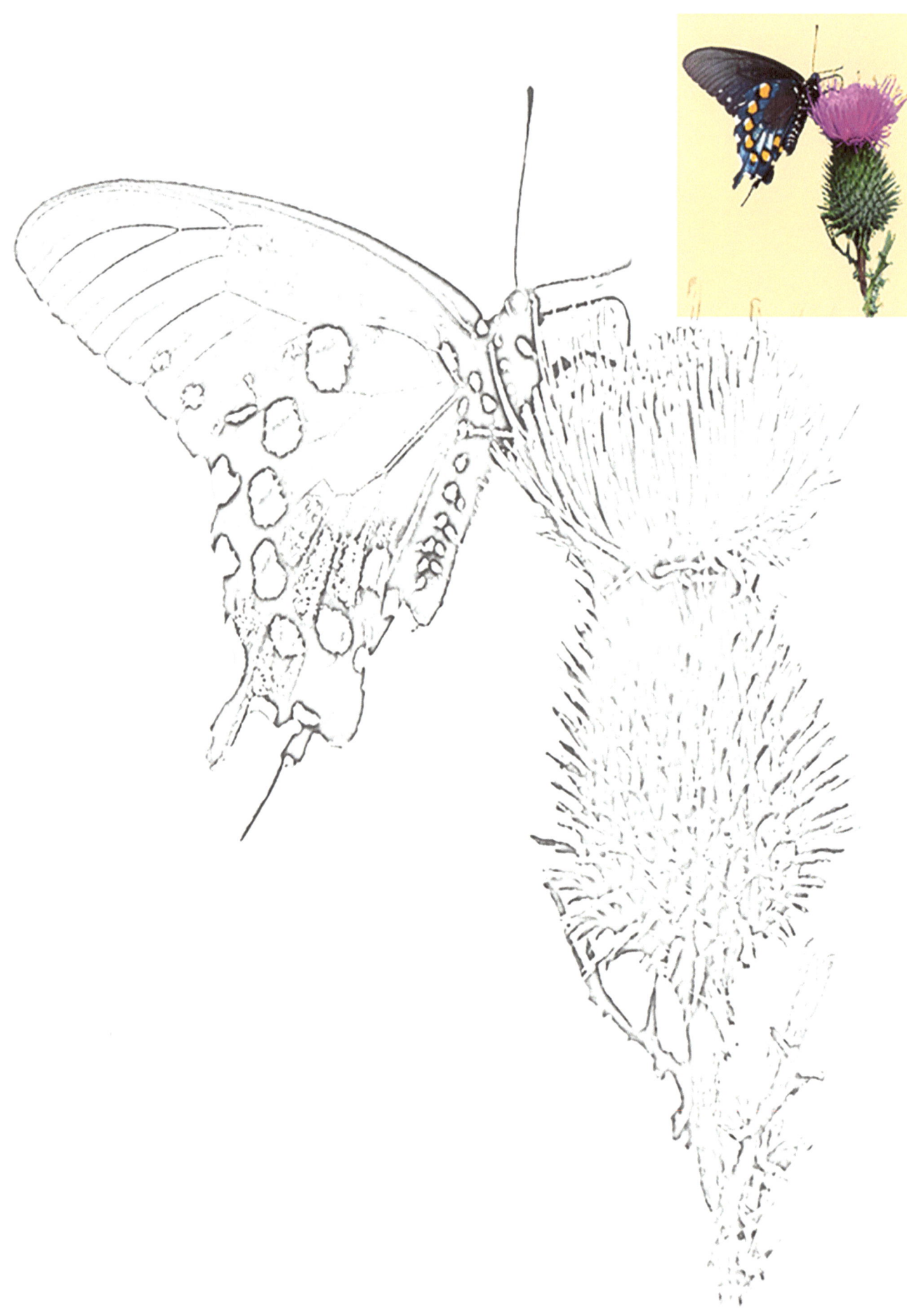

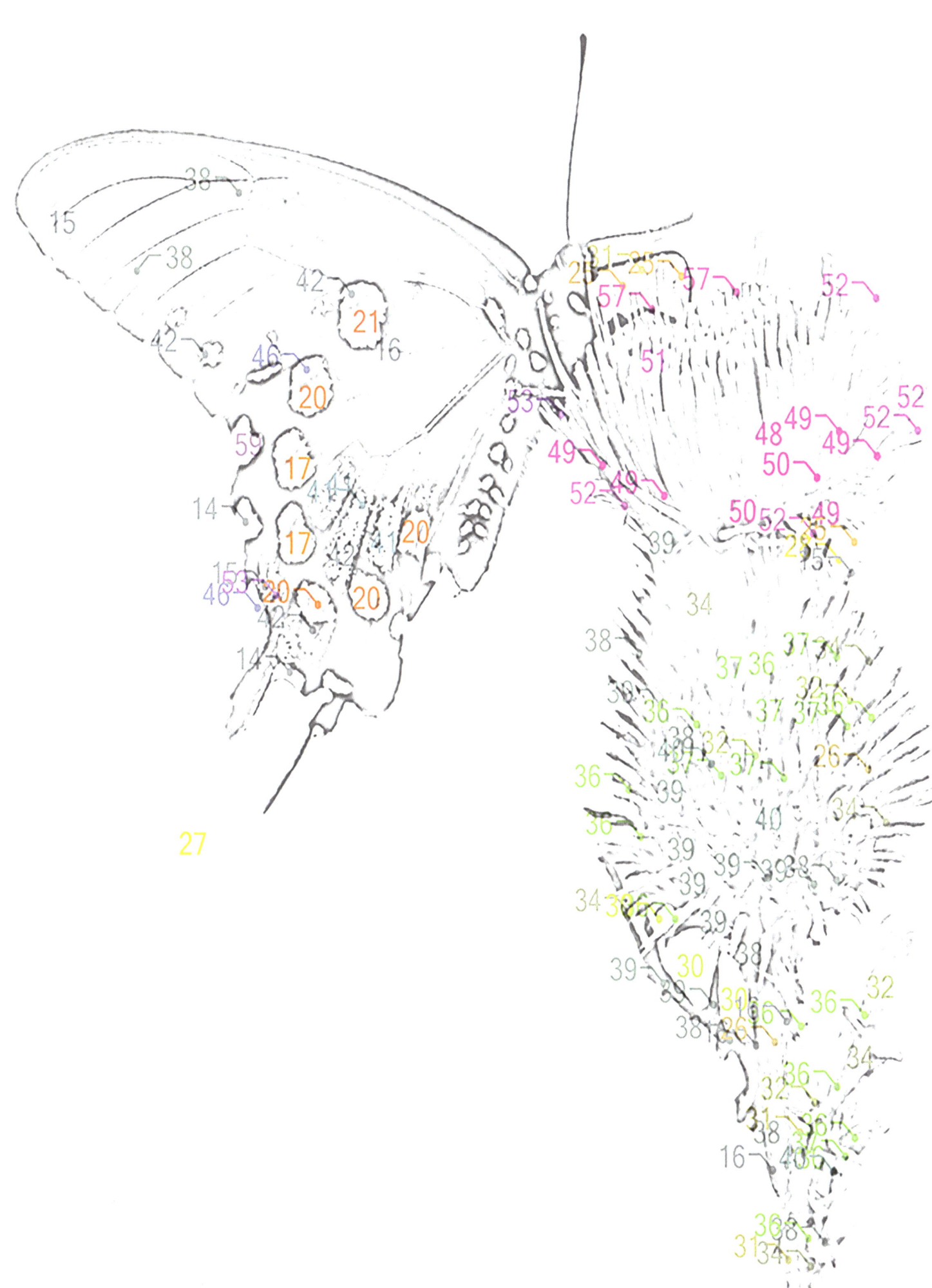

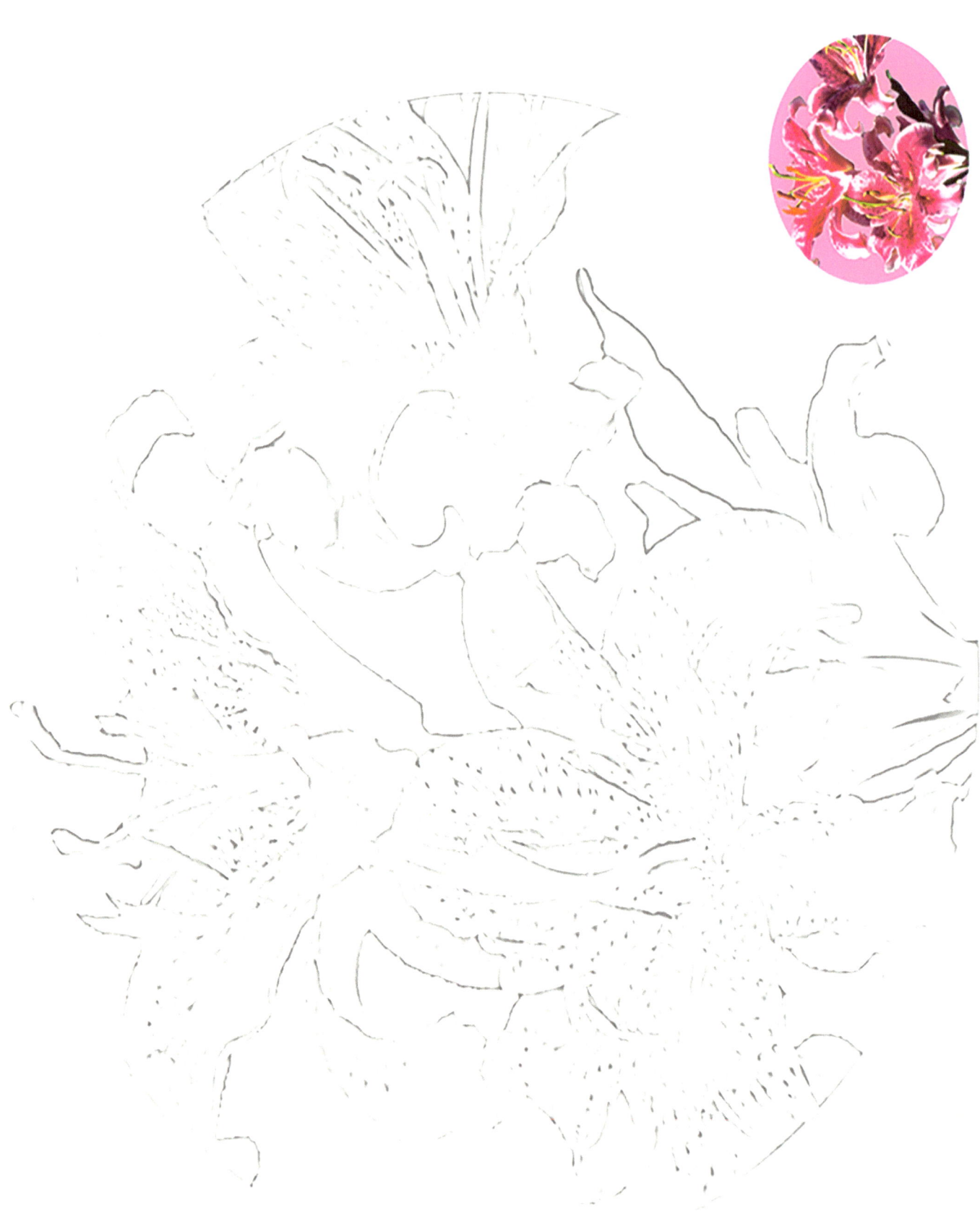

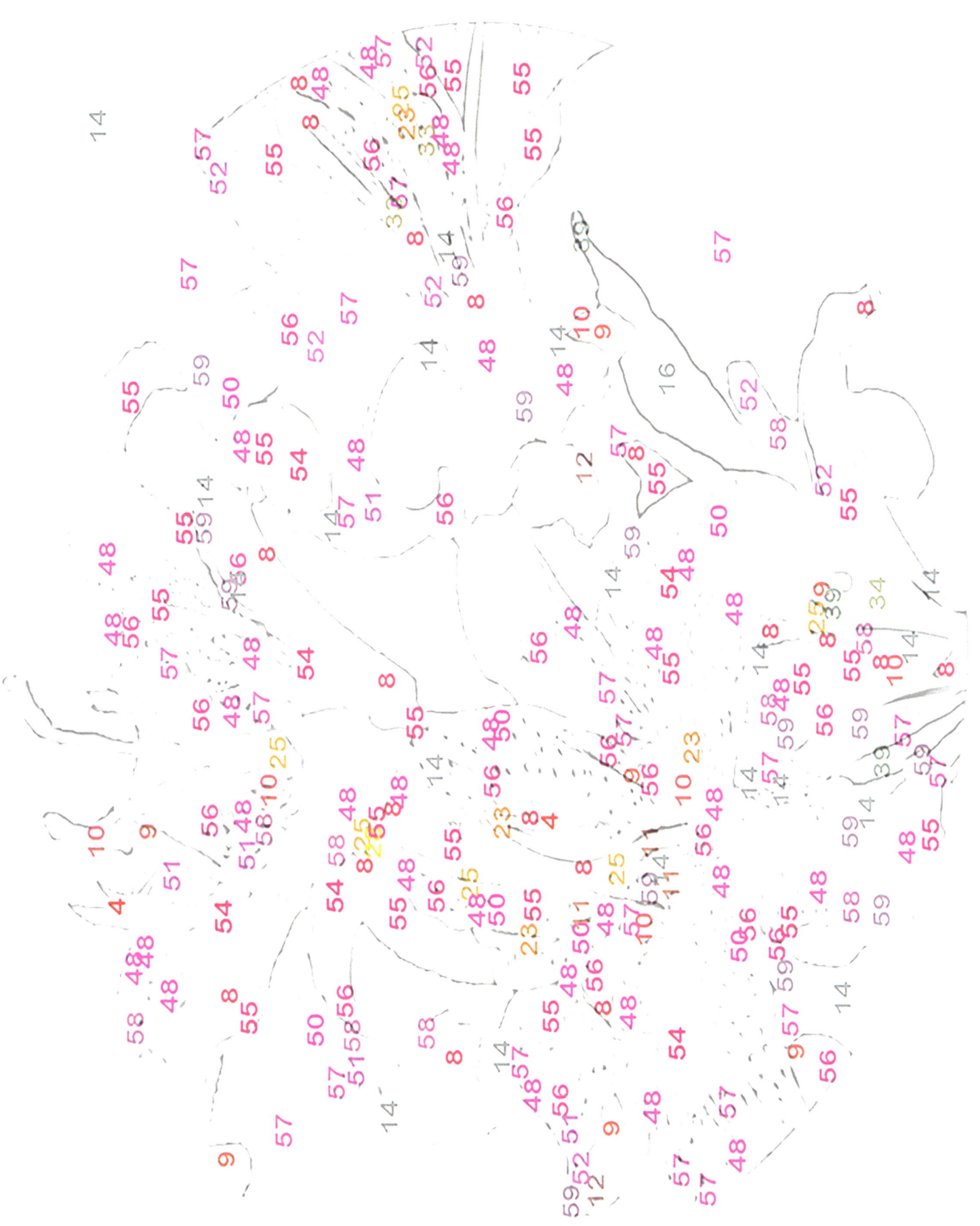

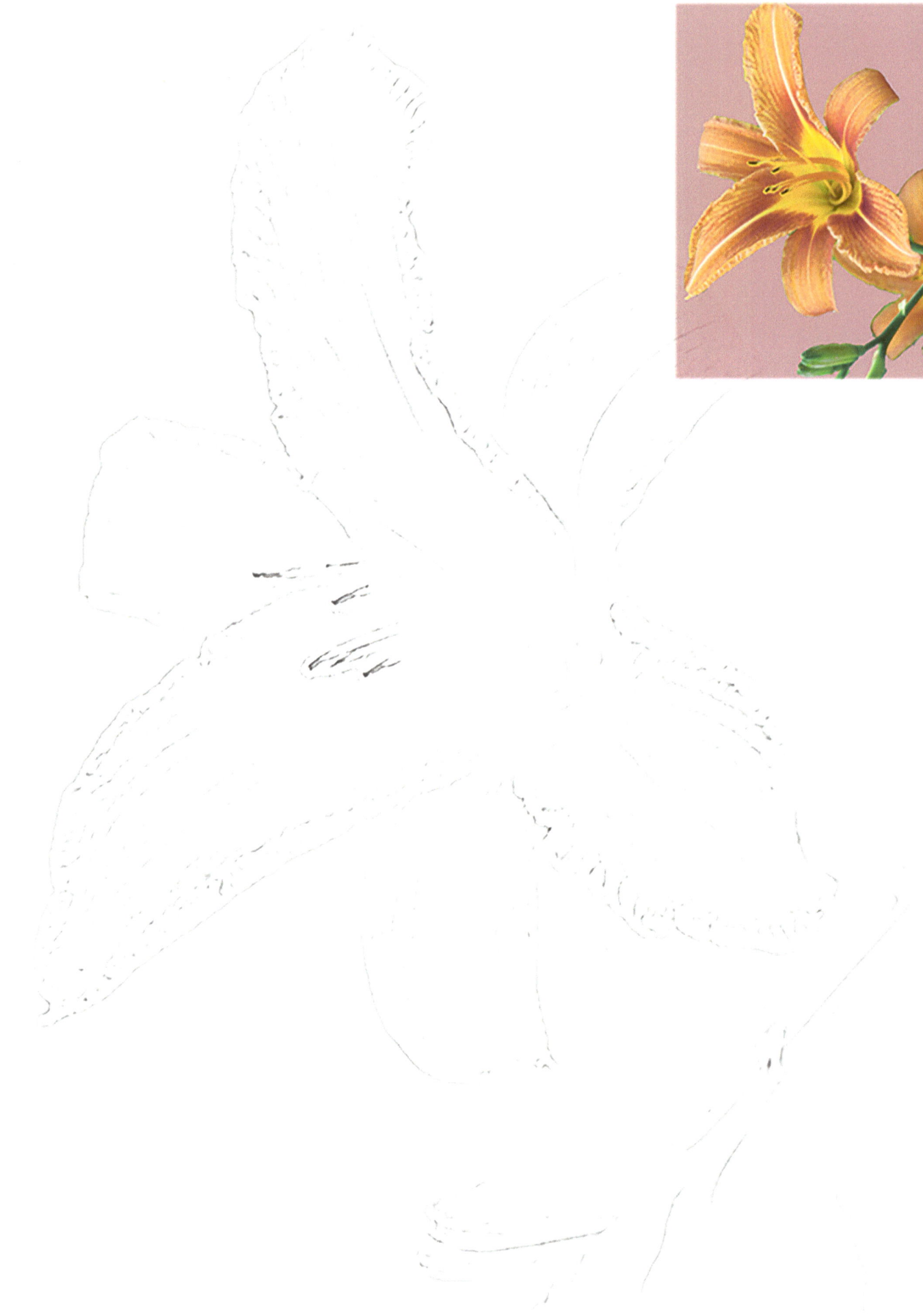

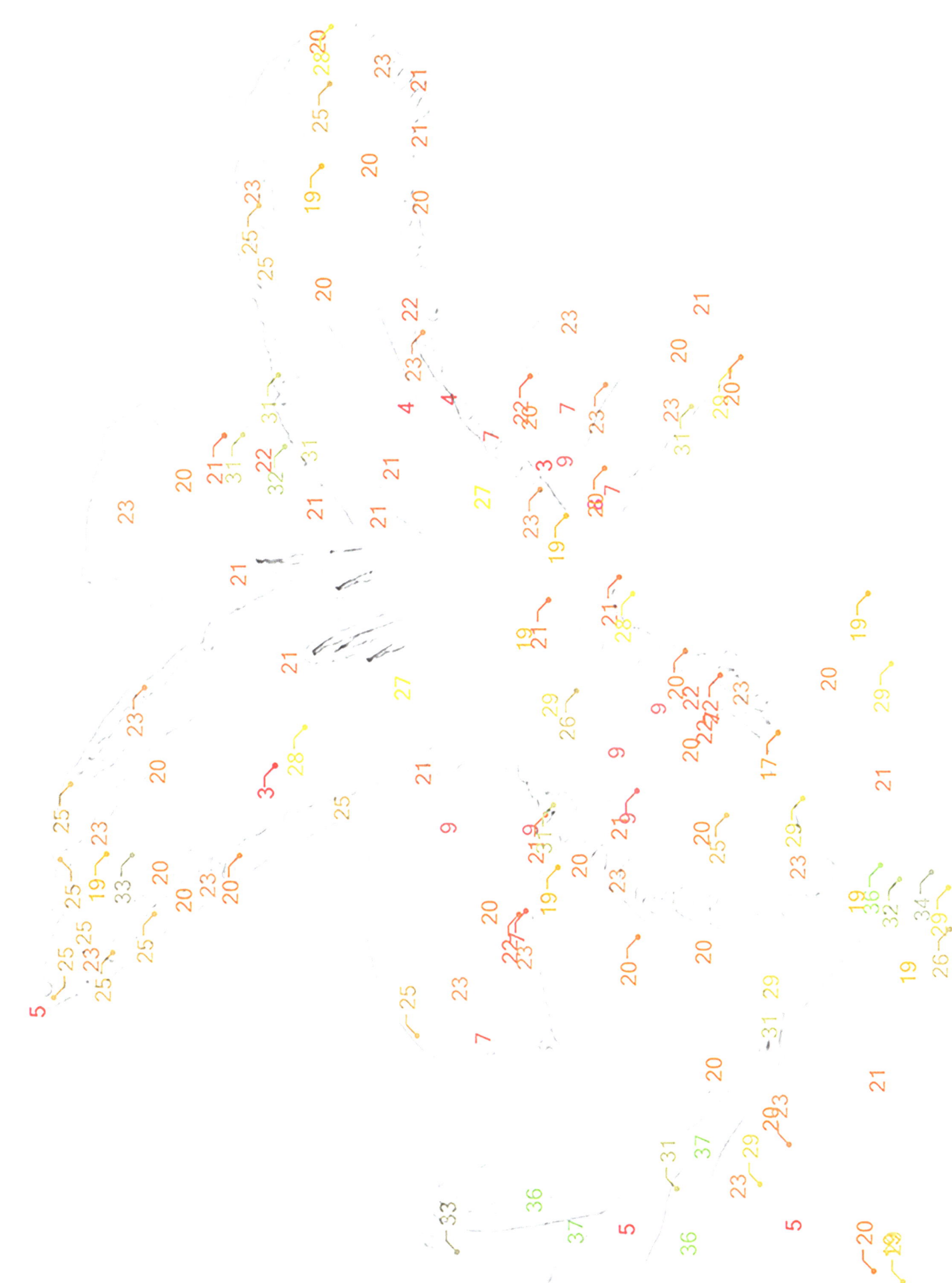

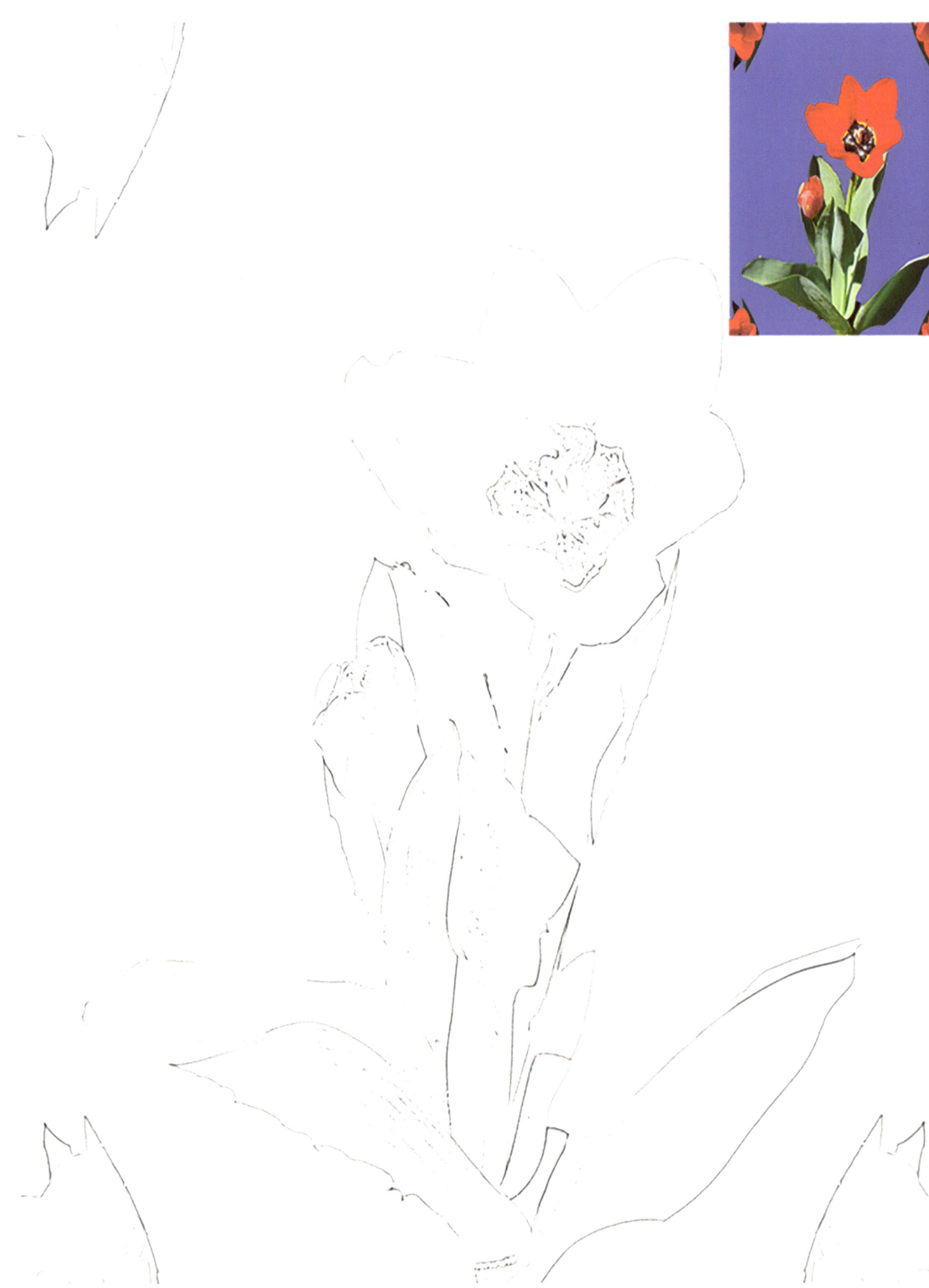

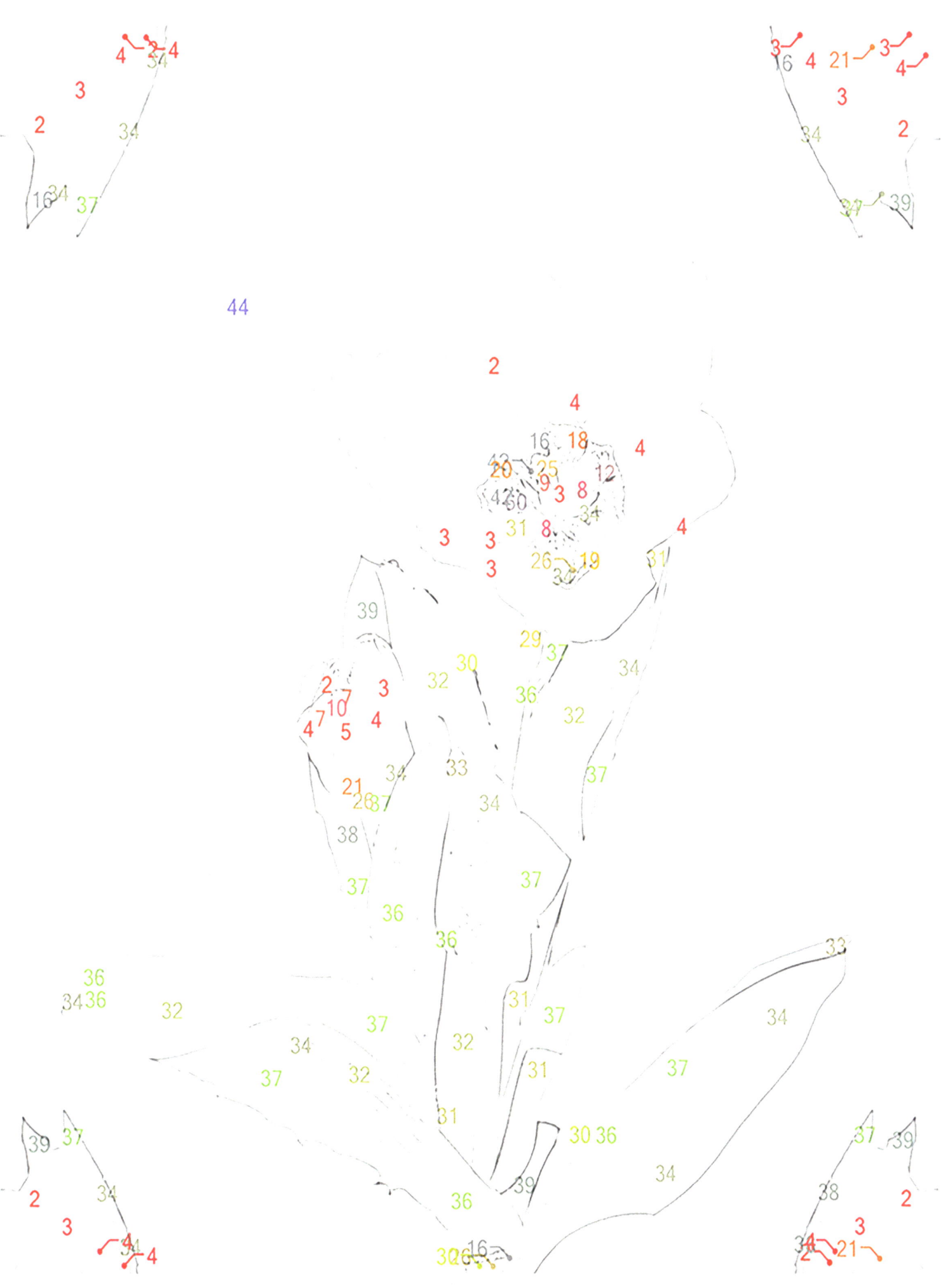

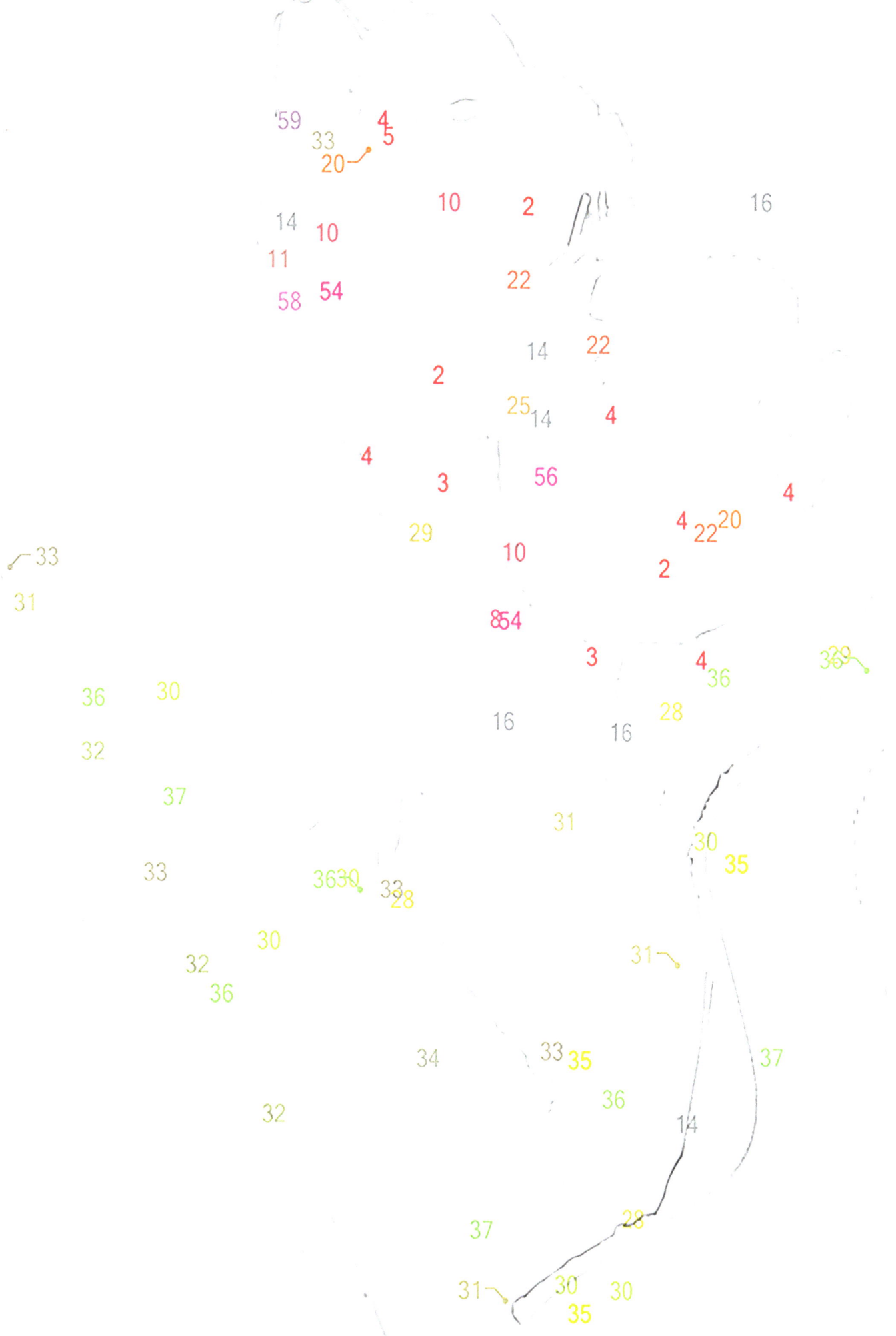

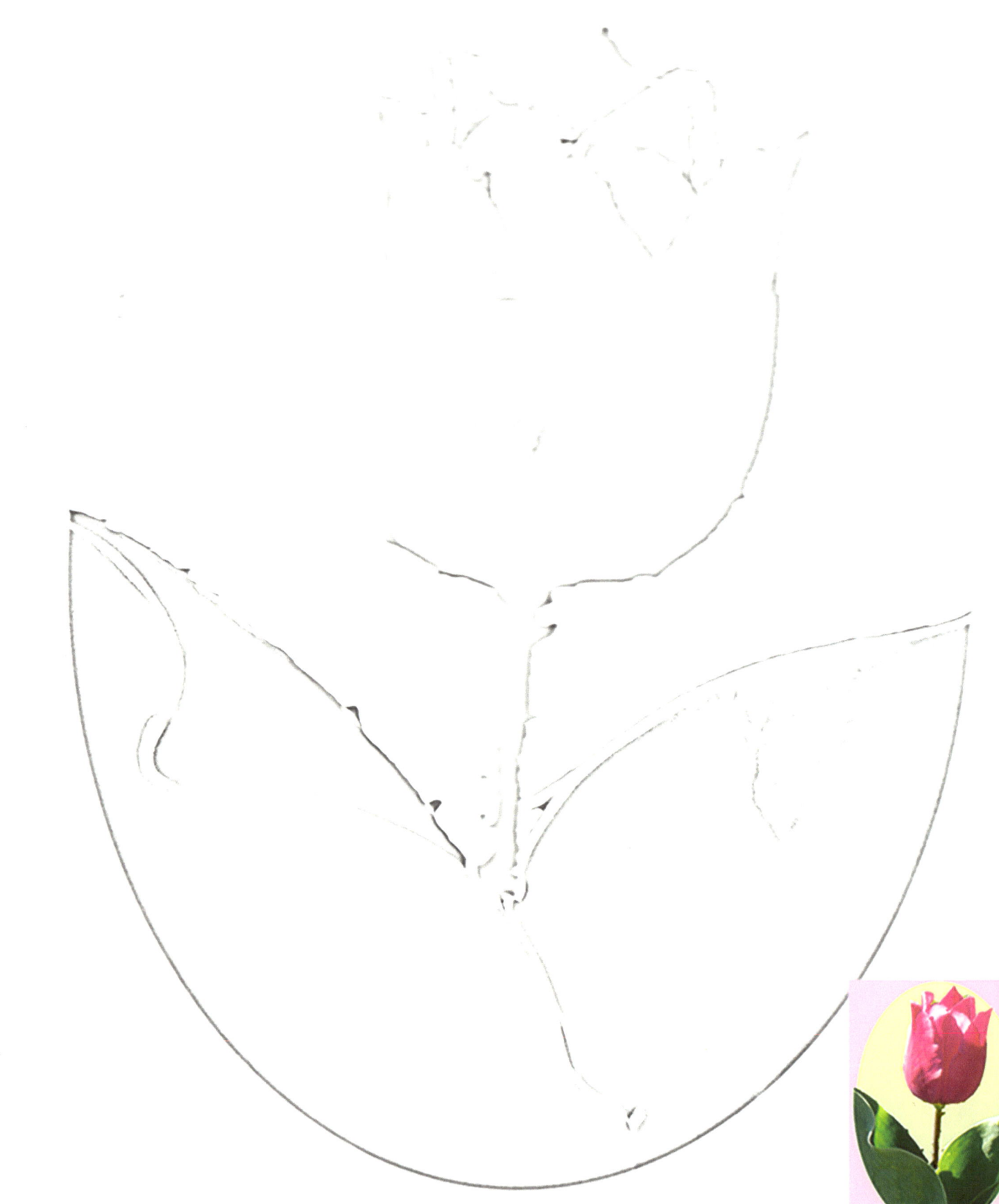

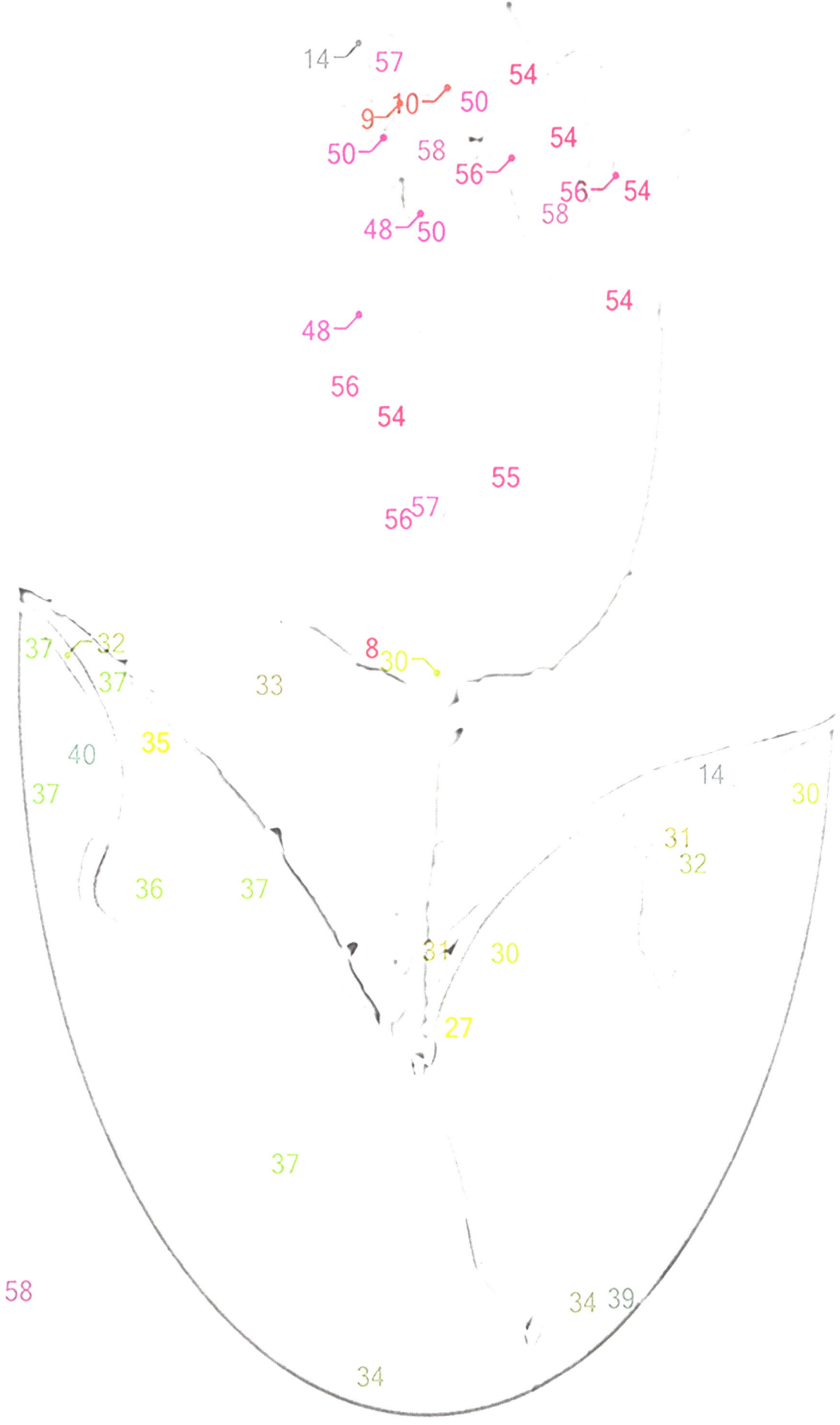

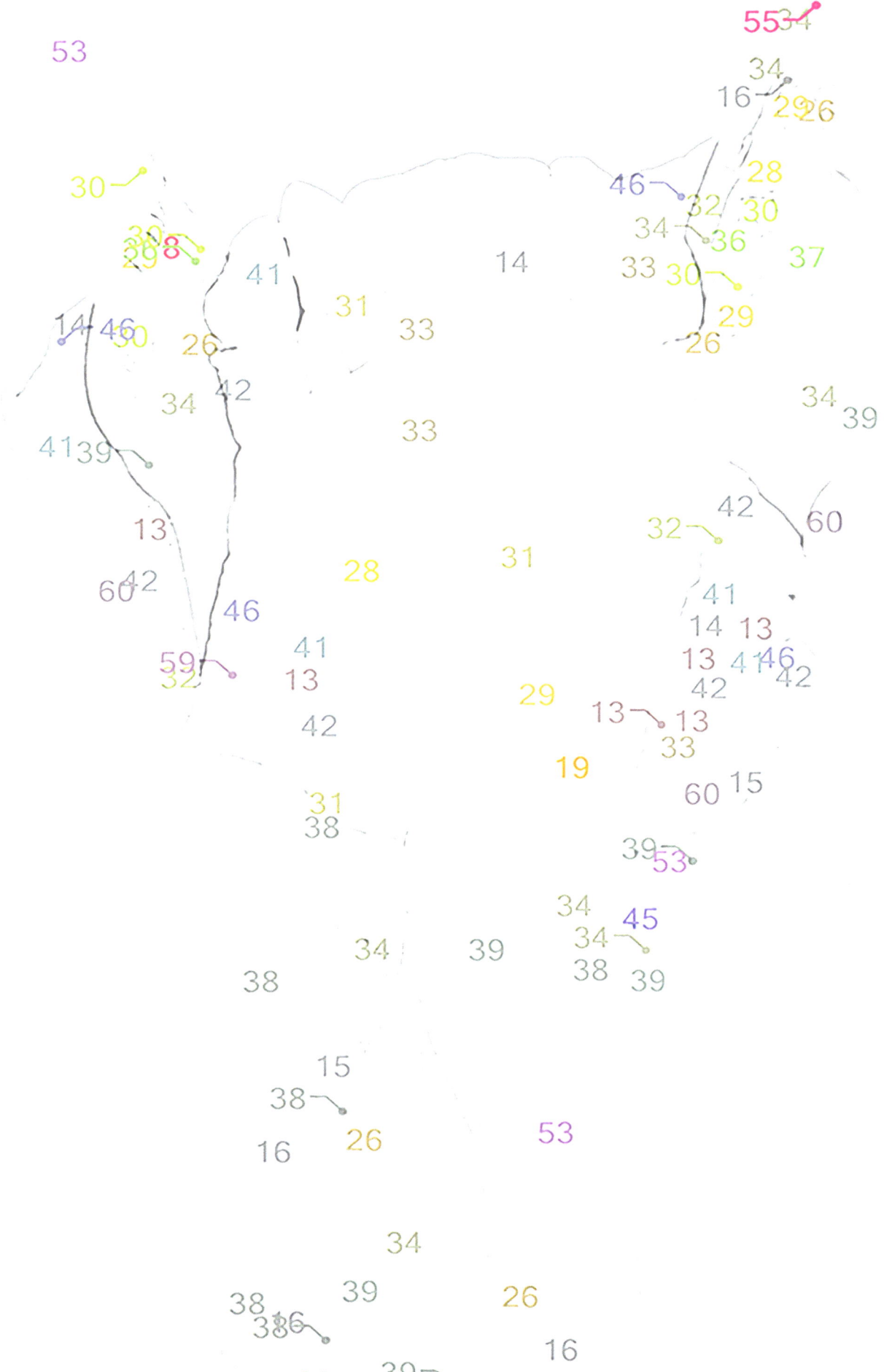